BUYING AND RENOVATING HOUSES FOR PROFIT

—— BUYING AND —— RENOVATING HOUSES —— FOR PROFIT ——

K Ludman & R D Buchanan

KOGAN
PAGE

Acknowledgement

Grateful thanks to Brian Healey of Villotel Ltd for travel arrangements, information and assistance in compiling the chapter on France.

First published in Great Britain in 1984
by Kogan Page Limited
120 Pentonville Road
London N1 9JN
Second edition 1988

British Library Cataloguing in Publication Data

Ludman, Kim, 1947-
    Buying and renovating houses for profit.—
    2nd ed.
    1. Great Britain. Houses. Purchase,
    conversion & sale —Manuals.
    I. Title   II. Buchanan, R.D.
    333.33'8

    ISBN 0-85091-727-2
    ISBN 0-85091-728-0 Pbk

Printed in Great Britain by
Biddles Ltd, Guildford

Contents

Introduction

When we wrote the introduction to the first edition of this book in 1984 it was against the background of a national economy ravaged by mounting unemployment. In 1988, happily, Great Britain seems to be poised on the brink of a new era of expansion so substantial that even the Japanese have remarked that 'the British disease is cured'.

As noted in the original introduction, buying and renovating old buildings can be a relatively secure and inflation-proof way of earning a living even in times of economic recession. It is obvious that in the current atmosphere of renewed confidence and financial growth, substantially larger profits are within the reach of the property renovator.

One of the most significant changes in the past four years or so has been the escalation in property prices. In 1984 it was possible to buy a run-down two-up two-down Victorian artisan's cottage in an up-and-coming part of London like Camden Town for around £35,000. Conversion to two units of accommodation cost around £20,000, and the resulting property could sell for around £75,000 (making close on £20,000 profit). Labour and materials costs have risen relatively slowly for a change, but the general increase in property prices plus the relative scarcity of such candidates for restoration would put the purchase of a similar dwelling at around £65,000—should one be available. However, this outlay would be more than offset by a possible selling price of £130,000 plus, against an only slightly heavier bill of £24,000 for conversion costs (yielding a profit of around £41,000).

As a consequence of such potential rewards—with both building societies and estate agents adding fuel to the fire by their readiness to offer larger loans on the one hand and to push up asking prices on the other—we are living in the age of the 'studio flat' and the 'London ripple'.

The studio flat syndrome is the result of the need for the cheapest possible accommodation for first-time buyers. As prices of even the most modest one-bedroom accommodation have soared, many buying their first home have been obliged to lower their sights. There has been a corresponding increase in what used to be called bedsitters—just one basic room for living, sleeping, food preparation and eating purposes. It's very much a result of the need to get a quart into a pint pot—one's own home despite the cramped conditions, that crucial first step on the ladder of property ownership which must be taken now in case the ladder goes beyond reach altogether. Taken to its extreme the studio flat becomes literally a broom cupboard—the current going rate in the West End of London is about £50,000 for 80 square feet. In other words, less and less is worth more and more.

The London ripple, the essence of which is the continually expanding area within commuting distance of London and the South East, occurs because many people are not prepared to compromise: in order to obtain the size of house they need or prefer they look farther afield from their workplace. The large London salary buys more space elsewhere, and ever-reducing rail travel times push the potential commuting distance up and up. Many people with higher salaries are so desperate to have a substantial family home out of town while retaining their income level that they use a pied-à-terre near work in the week and commute to and from the country pile on Friday evenings and Monday mornings. This once-weekly migration permits even greater distances from workplace to home, and carries the ripple effect still further. It also encourages enterprise in unexpected ways—one commuter who lives in a converted railway station in the West Country has a special arrangement with British Rail whereby the train makes a stop just to pick him up and drop him off again each day on his way to and from work!

Both the studio flat and the London ripple are good news for the property renovator. City, country, and all points in between provide more scope, with more backing available than ever before.

Should the aspiring renovator have moral objections to getting involved in the sardine-box end of the market? Not if he does it fairly. The asking prices for newly available properties are largely determined not by estate agents, building societies, vendor, builder or developer, but by collective market forces. If the vendor asks too high a price, the chances are the property will take longer to sell, and this in itself will cost him money—in more advertising, more time and effort and so on. He may end up reducing his price to a more acceptable level. If funds tied up in the project include borrowed monies he may even have to drop to a figure way below the going rate to get a quick sale to clear interest expenses. In practice it is possible to turn out even the most microscopic conversions with some style about them, and sell at a price acceptable to the market, the buyer and yourself.

A final query which comes to mind is 'When will it all end?'. When will house prices rise to such a level that no one can afford to move in? This is dangerous territory: in 1984 our introduction carried the embarrassing phrase '... it is unlikely that we shall see the kind of property booms where prices nearly double in three years...'. In the three years 1985-87 the London and South East market went up by 12, 15 and 20 per cent, while in Norfolk the figure for 1987 was nearer to 40 per cent in just one year!

The chairman of the Halifax Building Society said recently that the building societies did not think the ceiling had yet been reached, since while property prices in London were about five times the purchaser's annual income they were seven and ten times this figure in New York and Tokyo respectively. If the building societies go along with such ratios, the market is free to carry on rising.

The range of opportunities for imaginative property develop-ment continues to widen through the 1980s and on into the 1990s. More and more Brits are buying a first or second home abroad—in France (where prices in some areas are much lower than in Britain), Italy, Spain, Portugal, Switzerland, Austria, and so on—and several English estate agents deal in properties abroad. Also, home building societies are setting up branches in many foreign locations to service this growing market, and agents are arranging borrowing facilities from foreign banks. A considerable boost to this market is the increasing number of people who own one home in Britain and inherit another at their parents' death. The prefer-ence is often to sell the inherited property and buy a holiday home abroad, in some cases at a saving, particularly if it needs reno-vation. We have therefore included a chapter on property in France for these buyers and renovators abroad.

The market for the renovator has benefited, therefore, from this largely first-generation inheritance phenomenon: only now are the effects of relatively large-scale home ownership, as opposed to renting, starting to be felt.

Why property?

Restoring old houses keeps a large section of the building trade in lucrative employment. As a building grows older the more maintenance it needs and, although the evil day can be put off by the owner, when the time for repairs inevitably comes around, the bill is even bigger than it would have been for repairs carried out regularly.

Why, then, is this form of employment so much more secure than others? Because people must have houses to live in, and they demand a certain minimum level of comfort; this level may vary between different income groups but it remains constant through wide changes in the economic conditions of the country. For example, a high court judge and an assembly line worker, however different much of their daily lives may be, will both expect at the end of a day's work to go home to a comfortable, weather-proof home with central heating and pleasant decor. Even the tenants in council properties expect this, and usually get it. People have the need to feel secure and comfortable 'within their own four walls', so there is always a steady flow of people moving from rented accommodation to a place of their own.

The building trade is therefore a good source of income in relation to renovating older houses but it has its drawbacks. A competent one- or two-man building concern may earn a very good wage doing this kind of work but, owing to the nature of the operation, it is susceptible to loss of earnings due to bad weather and last minute changes of schedule by clients, on which one often has no redress. The small builder is more vulnerable to these problems than a craftsman employed by a large firm which can move labour to another project in the event of a delay of this kind, and so is his pay packet.

The solution to this problem is to buy, restore and sell properties. If you are able to do building work yourself (or even if not) this occupation will give you an income, during the course of each project, lasting several months. The problems encountered by the small builder will be avoided because *you* will be scheduling your work, not someone else, and delays on one job need not put a stop to progress; simply move on to another aspect of the renovation.

If an old property in need of repairs is purchased at a price appropriately below the market value of one in sound condition, one is then in a position to guarantee oneself work, and payment, over the period of time it takes to make it fit for sale at a profit. In other words, you can be a property developer!

Bricks and mortar have always been reckoned the most consistently reliable means of investment: better than savings, and more tangible and predictable than stocks and shares; once you have bought a property, it is yours. You can see it as proof of your investment, and do not merely have to rely on certificates or pieces of paper alone, as with so many others. A property investment has the advantage that the building which you have purchased will almost certainly start to increase in value from the moment you acquire it. This process will continue during your ownership irrespective of the renovation which you will be carrying out.

While it is unlikely that we shall see the kind of property booms where prices nearly double in three to four years, as in the last several decades, it is very seldom that property prices fall.

These, then, are two good reasons for the financial viability of the exercise.

Your suitability for the job

You will want to know, armed with the above information, how it can be of use to *you*.

You may be unemployed and you may know nothing about the building trade. How could it be possible for you to tackle a job like this?

Or you may already have a job which provides a steady income. Why would you want to branch out on your own and be self-employed? It's fair enough for someone who is already a bricklayer or carpenter, who simply wants to put their career in a stronger position, but a complete change of job may seem a bit drastic.

A moment's thought may help. *Anyone* who has a reasonable flair as a handyman could make a go of it, if he is prepared to put some effort into learning the various aspects of the job which we set out in later chapters. If you're not skilled in that area you could still supervise the work at any one of several levels of involvement, depending on what you really want out of it. This can range from being at the heart of the project in every way and at every stage, to merely putting up the capital and doing it as a spare-time activity.

Being out of work need not necessarily be an obstacle to becoming a property developer. Money is available much more easily than most people realise, if you organise the scheme well enough on paper to convince a potential backer—for example your bank manager or an enthused relative with spare cash to invest—that you mean business.

And if you already have a job, maybe your boss has just junked a dozen more of your brilliant ideas and you're thinking it's about time that all your creative effort should be used to greater effect.

If you're already self-employed, maybe you're stuck in the same predictable office routine day after day with no opportunity to meet new people; or you may be out on the road all day meeting too many new people and never spending enough time in one place.

Property renovation could be the thing for you in this case. As the kingpin in the project, you will have a good opportunity to set it up in the way *you* prefer to work, with as few or as many people involved as you wish (within reason). This activity gives plenty of free rein for one's ideas, a chance to meet a variety of people including vendors and purchasers of the properties you are involved with, considerable freedom in your daily movements (within the framework of work programmes), and a healthy balance of the indoor and outdoor life, physical exercise and mental effort. Instant access to the fresh air is quite a plus in any job.

Property renovation is one of the relatively few occupations which require no qualifications such as degrees, diplomas, City and Guilds etc. In fact, many of the people doing it are the kind who, while not stupid, do not really fit into this system. There is a lot of room for you if you like to be truly independent.

Such are the good points in favour of the work, but as with anything, there is the less attractive side.

If one is employing people one soon learns that there are some very tough, unhelpful and unreliable characters in the building trade. They can always be replaced, but it takes fairly strong character and determination to deal with the rogues and, in the course of your efforts to lift your house bodily out of the doldrums of neglect into the bliss of rebirth, you will have to do a lot of very hard, sometimes dirty work, much of it under pressure.

The key to success is the will to succeed, first and foremost. But this must be backed up by the right groundwork. The project for each property must be carefully prepared at the outset: research into areas for possible purchases must be thorough, and you must maintain the standard set for yourself at this stage right through until the property is resold, when you can take a (quick) breath. It means being prepared to keep working hard when it might seem very easy to stop.

The rewards, however, are immense. Apart from the steady, fulfilling employment during the course of the work, the potential for additional profits from the sale of the property plus the satisfaction of selling a home to people who are pleased to buy it from you add up to a pleasant feeling of achievement from a job well done.

Chapter 1
Starting

Having read the introduction you now have some idea of your suitability and aptitude for the business of property renovation.

The business comes under three broad headings of property purchase; renovation and conversion; selling/marketing.

Assets

One of the first things you need to do is to find out what you are worth. You must look carefully at your assets as these will play an important part in setting yourself up in business. Don't dismiss yourself as having 'nothing of value'. It is always surprising to find out what you are worth once you sit down and make a list of everything you own.

Assets can be cash; savings—which include building society accounts, premium bonds, local authority and other bonds; insurance policies; valuable articles such as antiques and jewellery, etc. Of course, you don't necessarily have to sell valuable items in order to raise money on them. If you own your own house then that is a valuable asset and will enable you to raise money in the form of a second mortgage. Friends and relatives with capital can also be an asset. (See Chapter 2.)

You may feel by now that you will have to give up everything you own in order to set yourself up in business. This is not the case. You merely need to know what you are worth so that you can decide how much of your own capital you wish to put into your business, and so that you can present a financial picture of yourself to others who may agree to invest in you.

Renovation or conversion?

Before you think about actually raising capital you will need to aquaint yourself with the housing market generally and areas in particular. Choosing the right property to buy is one of the most important parts of the project.

First decide whether you wish to convert into separate flats, or perhaps just to renovate and update a property as a single unit. Both schemes have their merits. Converting a property into flats will inevitably mean more work, more expense and more time. The advantage is that the rewards are usually greater. Also, when converting into flats you will need to make an application to the local authority for 'change of use'. This will involve a planning application supported by detailed drawings, for which you will need an architect. You will not be allowed to start any major work on the property until you have planning permission, which normally takes at least a few weeks, although in the meantime there are certain things you can be getting on with, such as external painting, pointing of brickwork, garden landscaping, etc.

Renovating a property as one unit (ie, restoring a house to its original condition), however, does not require a change of use application, and you would therefore be able to start work on it immediately. Plans do have to be submitted, however, if you intend adding bathrooms or altering drainage.

The advantages of being able to start work straight away are obvious. You will not be accruing interest unnecessarily on any loans you may have, and your initial enthusiasm can be used to the full.

You will have to decide for yourself which scheme to choose, but bear in mind that you will almost certainly make more profit from conversion into flats.

With this information in mind you can now pick an area.

Areas

There is a lot to be said for choosing an area that you already know, or better still, where you already live. The reason is that you will already be aware—maybe even without realising it—of the market generally. You will know roughly what houses are worth, and checking on a few that are advertised in estate agents' windows will help to confirm your assessment. You will also have some idea of the type of accommodation that is popular, whether flats, bedsits or large family houses. We ourselves found it much easier to operate in our own area because we had knowledge of local estate agents, we knew the location of builders' merchants and materials suppliers, which cut out a lot of unnecessary travelling—and supervision of the site was made much easier—very worthwhile especially if you employ contractors and are not always on the site yourself.

17

Nevertheless, if you decide to select an area you don't know, you must first research it very thoroughly.

You may be tempted, for example, to buy a property in a remote country area unknown to you. Some country properties, especially cottages, look ideal for someone starting a renovation business. They are also normally cheaper than properties in towns and cities. It is still possible to buy a really run-down but salvageable property for £10,000 to £15,000, but there has to be a reason why it is so cheap. It could be next to a glue factory or a pig farm, or there could be land subsidence.

Whichever property you choose to buy, you must be sure that you will have a market for it once you have spent thousands of pounds on modernisation. Also, you must gear the renovation to the type of market it will attract. In the case of country cottages, for example, too much money spent on too much renovation will price you out of the 'weekend cottage' market, which in some areas may be the only outlet for your property. So thorough research is important.

As a guide, we have listed the types of property which are worth considering, and those which you ought to avoid.

Best buys

In towns and cities

● Large, older properties, with garden if possible, which are in a generally run-down condition but are basically sound. These properties readily convert into flats comprising one, two or three bedrooms, and as many flats as possible should have use of the garden. Flats like these are always in demand, and a high proportion go to first-time buyers—newly married couples, etc: a very strong market.

To encourage first-time buyers, the flats need to be nicely converted with good separate access to each one, and have a sound basic standard of workmanship and finish. Avoid being too lavish. Goldfish ponds and sunken baths look very attractive, but the extra money you spend on installing them could put your otherwise very saleable flats out of reach of first-time buyers, and if you can't sell quickly you will be losing money.

● Small, older houses, again preferably with garden. Gardens are always a good selling point, as you will find when you come to market your finished renovation.

The smaller houses are usually two- or three-storey properties with two main rooms per floor and perhaps an extension at the back. As long as the house is basically sound (this means that no major underpinning or rebuilding of main walls will be necessary) the more neglected it is the better (and cheaper) it is for you to buy.

Small houses are more suitable for renovation and modernisation to make one living unit — ie, not flats — although the actual size and number of rooms is the key factor when deciding what you should do.

In order to make a small house attractive to buyers as a single dwelling, it is necessary to have at least two bedrooms of reasonable size and, if you can manage it, a third bedroom even if you can only just squeeze a single bed into it. You should be able to provide a bathroom (not just a shower room) as near as possible to the bedrooms, and a light, attractive kitchen.

With older period properties, interesting features such as fireplaces and ceiling cornices should be retained.

This type of house will generally be suitable for couples moving from smaller accommodation (flats), families, and single people moving upmarket (from flats, etc). So you should try to keep your potential buyer in mind when looking at properties, as this will be of benefit to you when you come to do the actual renovation work.

Just a word about large houses modernised to make one dwelling: there is a market for this type of property, of course, but people buying a large renovated house have a lot of money to spend and are going to be conscious of area and position and will want a very high standard of finish and decor. The capital outlay and the amount of work involved is likely to be too much for a first-time project — so we will forget them for the time being.

When looking at properties in towns and cities, try and imagine what it would be like to live there yourself. Keep in mind that people have to travel to work, buy food etc. A lot of people choose to come and live in an area because they can get to work easily. So when selecting properties to buy, look carefully at how close they are to bus and rail stations, shops, schools, parks etc, and try to avoid properties on busy main roads, which are often noisy and dirty. Most people would rather live in a quiet side street near amenities rather than on top of them.

Location is very important.

Country properties

As already mentioned, small country cottages are usually cheaper to buy than town properties. Suitable properties are:

● Secluded or remote cottages in a poor state of repair. Some cottages are so small that you will be able to carry out quite major work at a fraction of the cost of a similar project in town or city. But you must be careful not to spend too much in relation to what the property is worth, otherwise your mark-up (the difference between what you spend and what you actually receive after sale) is likely to be so minimal that the whole exercise will have been futile.

Country cottages will attract people looking for a second home or possibly a retirement home. In this situation people can afford to spend a long time looking for their perfect home as there is not the same pressure on them to move—in contrast with flats in towns and cities, for example, where buyers normally need to buy and move quickly, possibly because they have an existing property to sell, or they cannot afford the time off work anyway. So if you are tempted to renovate a country cottage, bear in mind that it could take a long time to sell and that your money will be tied up in it until it is sold.

● Houses in small towns and villages. These can be worth considering but again there is unlikely to be the pressure on people to buy. The market is not so clearly defined. The only certain way of assuring a sale is to have a buyer lined up before you start. The buyer can then specify his renovation requirements in advance. However, setting up a deal in this way means that, in order to protect you, your buyer will have to sign a contract agreeing to buy the property after renovation. If all this can be arranged it would be a very satisfactory deal for you as you will know all the costs involved, including the sale price.

Summary of best buys

● Houses in quiet roads in towns and cities, and near amenities. Detached, terraced or semi-detached and suitable for conversion into flats. Proximity to commercial area (eg, central London) along with good travel facilities.

● Any small house near a business or commercial area and amenities. Detached, terraced or semi-detached, and suitable for renovation as a single dwelling or conversion to small flats or bed-sit accommodation. Again, good travel facilities.

● Houses in areas which are starting to become fashionable—a lot of people will want to move into these areas.

● Country cottages within a few hours' drive of a city centre. They should be quiet and secluded but have easy access to major roads.

Other factors contribute to the suitability of a property. They are:
A garage—good selling point
On-street parking (no meters)
South-facing garden—gets a lot of sun
Cul-de-sac—no through traffic makes these streets pleasant to live in.

Summary of bad buys

● Houses in depressed areas. Prices will drop rather than improve. People are moving away because the area is no longer fashionable. You might be able to buy cheaply but you would never be able to sell at the price you required.

● Listed buildings. You would have to renovate them the way somebody else wanted—not the way you wanted. This is time-consuming and profit-losing. Buildings are listed because they have some architectural or historical merit and, if you want to alter them in any way, approval has to be sought from the listed buildings authority.
The same restrictions apply to a lesser degree in conservation areas. Conservation areas are declared by the local council when it wishes to retain the character and amenities of an area and control any development within it. Converting a property in a con-servation area will usually take longer and cost more, but it has to be said that many people like the benefits of living in such an area, so there would not necessarily be a problem in selling your prop-erty—only in converting it. Ask your local authority what would be required before you buy.

● Any property which is in an area that is going to be redeveloped on a large scale, or has major road improvements planned for it. Check with planning authorities.
Additional points to watch for:

Avoid main roads—especially very busy ones
Don't consider houses near factories/workshops etc
Don't consider houses a long way from shops and/or public transport
Avoid houses with major structural faults such as collapsed drains and foundations
Avoid houses adjacent to overhead railways.

21

Your legal position

In setting up your own business you will have to consider your tax position.

If you intend to work full time at property renovation, and work alone, then you will become self-employed (unless you are already).

Should you form a partnership with others you will probably consider forming a company, as this puts you and the others on a sound legal footing. You can either buy an existing company which has ceased trading, or set up a new one from scratch. Buying an existing company is cheaper, but you may have to change the memorandum and articles of association, which can cost money. Once the company is formed you will have to decide whether to be a company employee and pay yourself a wage, deducting tax under PAYE, or whether to choose self-employed status. Either way you can be a company director. Your accountant will advise which is best for you.

It is not a good idea to buy a going concern—ie, a company already trading in property renovation.

Whether you decide to work alone or with others, the following points are worth remembering:

● If you form a partnership with others they will want to be involved in decision-making. This can waste time and may mean that you disagree on working methods etc. So if you must form a partnership—keep the numbers as small as possible.

● A company will cost money and time to set up and run. Annual returns have to be made to Companies House. Returns for corporation tax have to be made and, as a property company, you will find it difficult to register for VAT. Certain home improvements such as central heating, previously zero rated, now attract VAT at the standard rate. You will also have to hold regular company meetings and produce minutes for which you will need a company secretary.

● Local authority grants may be harder to obtain as a property company.

● A definite advantage of a limited company is that it has limited liability. This means that in any legal action taken against your company, the claim is limited to the face value of the company shares, and does not involve you personally. Solicitors can advise on company law, more about which in Chapter 13.

● As a sole trader you will run the whole business yourself, the profit will be greater, and the day-to-day running of the business will be easier.

Any property you buy will have to be insured against damage, theft of materials and tools, and damage to persons and other property. Property insurance and public liability insurance are dealt with in Chapter 13, and are not as formidable as they sound.

At some stage you will need to appoint solicitors, who can do as much or as little as you want them to. It is likely that they will handle conveyancing (buyer's contracts, local authority searches etc) of your properties. They can also arrange the formation of your company, act as company secretary, and offer advice on any legal problems which crop up. (There are always a few.) If you already know a solicitor, all well and good. If not, then get some idea of charges and suitability and shop around before finally deciding.

The local authorities have laws with which you must comply. These are explained in Chapter 13.

You will also have to comply with the requirements of the District Surveyor (London), Borough Surveyor or Building Inspector (elsewhere). He is responsible for making sure that you carry out certain building work to the required standard, and his word is law—so don't upset him.

Presenting yourself

Whether you trade as a company or as an individual you are going to make contact with a lot of people and organisations. You will have to present yourself to banks, solicitors, council departments, materials suppliers and so on. To do this efficiently, business cards and printed letterheads are necessary. You will also need to write letters to many people, offices and official bodies, and for this purpose a neatly laid out letter on headed paper will present a professional image.

You will have to set up a company bank account, from which all transactions relating solely to the business should be handled. Most builders' merchants and materials suppliers will not take a company cheque unless you can produce company headed paper. In order to establish yourself with suppliers, you will need to become known, and the best way to do this is to present your card and headed paper when you buy materials. This way they will know that you are a bona fide trader with a registered company address, and will readily do business with you.

Chapter 2
Raising Capital

Having convinced yourself that the property business is right for you, the next thing you have to do is raise the money to start. If you have all the necessary capital to cover the outgoings on the whole project, this will maximise your profit; there need be no backers waiting for a share of the profits to diminish your own, and no bankers charging a steady interest rake-off on borrowed moneys.

Your own funds

It is always best to use your own funds, in whatever form, if you have them, rather than someone else's, which will always cost you.

Other sources

If you do not have all the money you will need, or even if you have none at all, there are several other sources. These fall into three categories:

- Backers and partners
- Loans
- Grants.

Backers and partners
Family. There may be members of your family sufficiently keen on the new project to help with some of their savings—you may be surprised to find that a great aunt has been wondering how to reinvest her premium bonds, and only bothers to tell you when she hears of your proposed enterprise.

Friends. You may find that a friend is prepared to put up some of the front money to get you started once you show that you have thought the whole thing through well enough beforehand; try it out, even on the ones who you think will not show any interest—

enthusiasm is infectious even to the cynics, and after you've let them shoot you down in flames a few times, they will be impressed by your persistence if you press on with your plans despite what *they* may consider to be impossible odds. In fact they may well end up putting *their* money where *your* mouth is!

Contacts. If you put the word about among your friends and acquaintances you may well get to hear of someone who is looking for a project to invest money in. It is surprising just how much investment capital is available, but you won't get to hear about it by day-dreaming of yourself as a property magnate and complaining, as so many do, that your talents are not appreciated. *Show* these talents by your efforts to interest people in the venture. Remember that at this stage of the game you will be learning your most difficult lesson—how to present a case involving quantities of money which most people only dream about—but your nervousness about it will be reduced by the relaxed way in which people who are used to putting up considerable sums as backing discuss your problems with you. Pick up on their air of assurance and get to grips with their ways of looking at your 'baby', and you will begin to feel more at ease with what, not long before, may well have seemed even to you a hare-brained scheme.

You will almost certainly turn up some positive results in this area. You must come to an agreement with your backer as to how much return you will give him or her on the investment. One way to arrive at this figure is to arrange to make the backer's share of the profits proportional to his initial stake in the venture; this need not mean that if he puts up, say, 30 per cent of your total capital that he is entitled to collect 30 per cent of the profits. He has a right to expect a greater return on his money than he would get from the safest forms of investment, ie building society or bank deposit accounts (at around 12 per cent gross per year), for he is undeniably taking a greater risk with your venture, but he should also take into account the fact that, in the early projects, you must find your feet financially. It could be that if you commit yourself to giving him a fixed sum at share-out time, before the project starts, the payment of this money on resale of the house leaves you out of pocket.

To summarise: agree on giving backers a share of the profits proportional to their original stake (but trimmed a little to take into account your greater involvement; eg, if you have three backers contributing say 50, 25 and 12 per cent respectively, offer

25

them 40, 20 and 9.6 per cent. This enables you to collect the difference at the share-out, 17.4 per cent of the profits, as a reward for your efforts).

Arrange, if possible, for the profit each backer will receive to be more than he would get with a building society or bank, so if your scheme ties his money up for three months you should offer him more than 3 per cent on his investment. But make sure in your calculations that this is feasible—more about this later.

You should decide at this stage whether to formalise any of these arrangements. Experience tends to show that it is always safer for all concerned to draw up a legal document, form a legally binding partnership or a limited company which commits everyone to the enterprise not only in spirit but also in responsibility. This applies just as much to a joint venture with a close relative as with a more formal, professional body such as a bank.

Sleeping partners. Although raising all your cash from sleeping partners, ie backers who merely contribute their share to the project at the outset and wait for their profit at the end of the job, may seem the best approach, in practice it is difficult for these people to stand aside and resist the temptation to pitch in their own suggestions on how the work should be carried out. This is natural enough, since they probably feel that their money will be that much better looked after if they 'help you' to utilise it well. Hence, the more sleeping partners you have, the greater the risk of the project becoming a tug of war. These problems will be compounded if you also have a poorly defined business relationship because you started out being such close friends.

Working partners. In practice, it may be better to take on at least one working partner. He or she, in addition to contributing a stake, can help with the work and the running of the job.

Difficulties which sometimes arise in joint decision-making in a 50-50 set-up of this kind can be more than offset by the sharing, and hence lightening, of the burden of keeping the job moving. It is really up to you to decide exactly how to tackle this problem of partners and backers, depending on your particular situation and preferences, but the issues mentioned above will help you to consider the most important aspects.

Loans
The most readily available loans for the renovator are from banks and building societies. These organisations are both useful sources

of funds but, of course, the money which you borrow from them will be subject to interest charges from day one. Whereas a backer will charge you nothing for the use of his money *during* the project itself, a bank will almost certainly be charging interest daily on borrowed finance and deducting it from your account every three months. This means that any delays during the course of the operation will add to your costs accordingly. However, it is easy to raise money by this means, and the very act of setting about doing it is a healthy astringent to the euphoria which sets in as the project draws nearer to becoming a reality.

Banks. Most bank managers will be very ready to listen to your proposals, but will not contribute all of the funds. They will want to see financial projections (discussed in Chapter 7), and they will expect you to be putting up some front money. One way of doing this, if you have no available capital, is to get together with several partners, each of you contributing an equal stake to a kitty. This kitty can be used as 'share capital'. Form a limited company with your colleagues. Your combined funds in the company represent a measure of commitment and show your ability to get the thing together, and when shown this evidence, your bank manager will be prepared to match this money with two or maybe three times as much.

If you or your partners do not have enough money to make the initial kitty large enough for you to raise all the finance you need by this method, each of you should apply for individual personal loans, or unsecured loans, which are reasonably easy to obtain if you are a householder: you may have to sign a few forms, but you need not commit yourself to signing away the roof over your head or anything drastic. It is still best to go through the banks rather than other means of obtaining credit, as these (ie credit card organisations, etc) charge exorbitant rates of interest.

Thus the money *can* be raised through the bank, though it may be diplomatic to choose as your company bank a different one from that which has provided the unsecured loan(s); if one of your number has no need to borrow his stake, put the company account with his branch.

Your bank manager may prefer you to take out a secured loan or he may offer you an overdraft. If you are already self-employed you may have an existing arrangement with the bank which permits you to overdraw, that is, go into debit on your account up to a pre-arranged limit. It may be possible to extend the limit of this overdraft for the renovation scheme, though do remember that an overdraft facility can be withdrawn without notice. However, it is not a common practice.

With a secured loan you stand a good chance of being able to raise a greater sum of money, but the bank will have a tighter hold over you; the manager will probably want to take a second charge on property which you already own. This means that, should he have any difficulty collecting repayments from you, he *could* recoup the money by claiming a share of your home and demanding it be sold so that he is repaid. This is really only a formality, and the chances of any such uncomfortable proceedings are very remote.

In the case of secured and unsecured loans, and one form of overdraft, repayment is made on a regular (usually monthly) basis, the repayments consisting of principle and interest. The period of repayment is pre-arranged, as is the amount of each instalment. If you run into difficulties, or want the borrowing carried over a longer period, the banks are ready to listen and quite flexible in their approach.

Where you are working on an overdraft allowance the permissible borrowing limit remains the same for the duration but, more important, you will only be charged interest on the amount you are in debit at any given time: unlike loans, the money need not be drawn until the moment you need to use it, so if there are delays you will not be parting with regular repayments which may be hard to find. Also, if you have sources of income other than the renovation, paying these moneys into your overdrawn account will reduce the drain of interest. You do not *have* to make regular repayments anyway with this arrangement, as long as you keep below your limit, although in practice it's best to try to do so.

If all of your finance for the project is borrowed—the funds provided by the bank to your *company* account will almost certainly be on an overdraft allowance basis—it goes without saying that speed will be of the essence in completing the project to keep outgoings on interest payments to the lowest possible level. The *high street banks* also give mortgages on property. The process of securing a mortgage is the same whether through a bank or building society (see below).

Building societies. Of the other possible means of borrowing, a remortgage or second mortgage is one of the best. If you own a property you can raise capital by mortgaging it for the necessary sum with a building society.

Even if your property is already mortgaged, it may be of sufficient value to enable you to increase the mortgage: the property will probably have increased in value since you purchased it, so that even if you obtained the highest mortgage possible then, its present market value will permit more borrowing by this method.

Venture capital

This is financial backing from organisations funded by wealthy clients who have income to spare and wish to gamble a little. Some venture capital organisations have a narrow band of interests—many concentrate on backing companies developing new technology such as computers and medical research equipment—but others, including many merchant banks, have a wider brief. Some venture capital fund managers seem to have carte blanche. The rules which they apply may be more flexible than the average high street bank or building society, and more dependent on their gut feel.

Venture capital is likely to become a vital source of funding for more kinds of business enterprises as it gains ground. As a property renovator you should not rule it out as a possible source of finance. Although the minimum figure most companies will consider supplying is around £100,000, smaller deals are possible if you hunt around. The British Venture Capital Association will supply you with a free directory giving details of its members and the sort of activities they specialise in. Their address is: 1 Surrey Street, London WC2 2PS; 01-836 5702.

A word of warning here: although no personal borrowing on your own part may be required, the investors may want a share of the profits from your venture and expect to muscle in on the management side of the proceedings. The venture capitalist's managerial competence in the client's field of activity may not match his ability to provide cash, so give this source of finance some thought before deciding on it.

Equity release loans

A relatively new development (1988), is the equity release loan which enables you to borrow against the value of a property which you own outright or have a mortgage on. It is like a mortgage in that it is repaid over a similar period—between 15 and 30 years—hence keeping repayments much lower than those on the typical bank loan, which is usually over three to five years. But it differs from a mortgage in that borrowing more on your property does not require the 'buying out' of a previous mortgage on the property. For example, if you had a mortgage of £30,000 on your home and wished to raise an additional £20,000, with equity release you would simply borrow another £20,000. To do this via a mortgage would necessitate taking out a new £50,000 mortgage on the property and paying back the first mortgage.

Equity release loans are simpler and more convenient than mortgages for many reasons. One of the most important is that when you decide you would like to repay the loan, equity release simply requires repayment of the £20,000 and then you are back to the original £30,000 mortgage. In contrast, with an increased mortgage of £50,000 to service the additional £20,000 borrowing, to repay your additional £20,000 borrowing you would have to take out a new £30,000 mortgage in addition to paying back the money. This is more time-consuming, expensive, and confusing than simply repaying an equity release loan.

It's worth shopping around the banks and building societies for both mortgages and equity release deals as, despite what the television ads would have us believe, some managers seem relatively unwilling to lend to the selfsame applicants as others welcome with open arms. There are many other methods of raising your capital but for various reasons they are less practical, for example, borrowing from finance houses. The only real alternative which may be available to you is a grant.

Home Improvement Grants

There are several types of local authority home improvement grants. The two most important categories are:

- Mandatory Grants
- Discretionary Grants

You are automatically entitled to a Mandatory Grant, which is described as being a grant for 'basic improvements and associated repairs', if your property meets certain universal basic requirements. Discretionary Grants are only given after your particular case has been considered on its own merits and depend on the local availability of funds. The waiting list for Discretionary Grants is likely to be about 12 months (before the awarding of the grant, not payment of the money!).

Priority is given to the Mandatory Grants, which can help pay the costs of installing a fixed bath or shower, wash-hand basin, sink, inside toilet and hot and cold water supplies where these facilities do not already exist.

The amount of money you will qualify for is based on a set of tables which are published by the DOE in Housing Booklet No 14. This is very lucid and strongly recommended reading. Each item of work is allocated a sum of money in the tables. This represents the 'eligible expense limit', ie maximum expenditure that the DOE thinks is reasonable on the work. The amount of money awarded in the grant is then a *percentage* of this figure (75 per cent at the time of writing). Any expenditure over and above this figure will have to be financed by you.

Conditions attached to grants

Local authority grants for home improvement can be a source of considerable finance but there are two major drawbacks.

First, work must not be started before the grant is awarded, which can mean a wait of two or three months, sometimes longer. Funds from this quarter cannot be relied upon when planning the project, for local authorities often work in mysteriously inconsistent ways. So dicey is the grants system that an acquaintance of ours who has been renovating houses for 15 years has never bothered with them in all that time: remember—if work is held up while you are waiting for final confirmation of the grant, valuable time and money may disappear down the drain with nothing accomplished.

Second, even if you have been able to arrange a grant in record time, maybe before purchasing the property, or if you have been fortunate enough to purchase a property for which a grant (and probably planning permission) has already been obtained by the vendor, the grant money will have to be paid back to the authority if it decides that your renovations are purely a means to the end of reselling the premises as a profit-making venture. At best it is then merely an interest-free loan (but at a price even so—count the hours you end up spending on it, and remember that time is money in this kind of exercise).

There is only one circumstance in which you may keep the grant. If the property is the only one you own, and you are working as a private self-employed individual (or doing the work in your spare time while having another, full-time, job) rather than operating as a limited company, you are less likely to be regarded as undeserving. If you can persuade the authority that you are not specifically renovating for profit—you may want to renovate one house only in the foreseeable future, and sell it after living in it for 10 years or so—there is every chance the authority will not reclaim the grant.

Some councils require you to sign a declaration when applying for a grant; this commits you to paying back the money if you move house within a period of five years (the same period applies throughout the country), although, yet again, interpretation of these rules seems to vary; we know of two contradictory cases which prove the point.

In the first, someone residing in a flat on which she had a mortgage was reluctantly obliged to drop her application for a roof repairs grant because she could not be sure that she would not be moving within the statutory period.

In the second, on the other hand, someone who had sold his own house and bought one to renovate specifically for profit was given a very substantial grant. He subsequently sold the house at a not dissimilar profit, and no claim was made on the grant by the council!

There does seem to be some evidence to show that the local authority, and the taxman, are prepared to go along with this arrangement if it only happens once. Once it becomes a routine though, if house after house is bought and sold with grants used to fund the restoration, council and taxman alike will be at your door for money. You will be regarded as part of 'the private sector', and as such a profit-making concern, undeserving of the ratepayers' assistance. This is really fair enough and observes the general spirit in which local authority aid and the tax laws were drawn up.

To summarise the above, the only means by which you may use grants on a regular basis are:

- If you live on the premises and/or the property is the only one you own.
- If you do not sell it until the five-year period has elapsed.

This arrangement may be useful to you, although it is unlikely to provide sufficient income if purchase and renovation provide your sole means of employment. Nevertheless, if you are a writer, artist, actor or musician, for instance, or are for other reasons prepared to put up with a subsistence wage for the opportunity it gives you to allocate some of your time to another activity, the freedom to juggle your timetable around may justify the relatively modest returns to be had. But remember that such a drawn-out project is not a good candidate for financing with loans, as the interest charges over such a long period are prohibitive.

It may be possible, even if you are conducting your business as a limited company, to qualify for a grant on *one* of your properties, but one only. If you should get to the stage where you are renovating several properties at once, there is nothing to stop you treating one of these as your own home, applying for grants for it, restoring it and hanging on to it before selling at a profit after five years. In practice you will probably have to live in it anyway, as unoccupied it will be prone to vandalism and will not be paying its way, apart from the ethical objection that habitable dwellings should not be left unoccupied when housing is in such demand. Your grant-aided property will probably have to be run with a separate bank account from the company account to simplify accounting procedures. This is discussed in Chapter 15 under *Using profits*.

Other grants

There are other more remote possibilities under the loose description of grants:

Government aid for small businesses. Complicated.

Department of the Environment (DOE) grants for refurbishing buildings of special historic value. These properties often have striking architectural features—pilasters, colonnades, porticoes etc, and some are centuries old. Applications for Historic Buildings grants present even more of an uphill battle than for Home Improvement grants. The DOE tells us that general policy is to discourage such applications since it is felt that the condition of these properties is reflected in a low purchase price, which is in itself a sufficient perk! Clearly, funds are limited and go only to the really desperate cases.

The government Youth Training Scheme. You may be tempted to kill two birds with one stone here, availing yourself of a couple of young labourers at the government's expense while helping to reduce the numbers of the nation's unemployed in your own small way. Don't. You will have more than enough on your plate without taking on someone who is new to the world of work and another pile of paperwork to be dealt with.

Chapter 3
Which Property to Buy?

How do you decide which place to buy? There are several points of which you must make yourself aware.

The local property market

What is the state of the property market in the area where you want to renovate? Are prices on the increase as a result of great demand, or is the locality already flooded with homes for sale, depressing prices as a result?

Tour the local estate agents' offices

This will enable you to look at details of properties on the market — photographs, written descriptions of layouts, numbers of rooms and dimensions will help to familiarise you with what's available. You will soon see that only a small percentage of the properties for sale will fit all the parameters which you must apply, and not least of these is the overall budget for the project. You must base everything else in the project on the budget, from how much you are prepared to pay for the house through the total estimated cost of the work, to other expenses such as solicitor's, surveyor's and architect's fees, and loan interest.

Another vital aspect to check out at this stage is the possible need to apply for permission for a 'change of use' for the premises, and for planning permission.

Have you found a suitable property?

Does the house you have in mind for the project (there will probably be one or two which started you thinking of renovating in the first place) lend itself to improvements and/or alterations without an exorbitant outlay of time and money? Is the end product capable of yielding an adequate profit after all overheads are taken into account (possibly including the interest on loans from banks which will continue to be charged, even when work is completed on the property) until such time as the investment is recouped by resale?

Factors in your choice

Budget

In order to minimise the risk involved (for with any business venture there is always a risk) it is best to keep to as low a budget as possible with the first project. Save the more ambitious possibilities—digging out a basement to put in an extra flat if you are converting, or adding a roof extension to provide another—until you have found your feet on the basics.

The total amount of money needed to finance the operation will depend, first, on the cheapest typical price for a run-down property of the type which lends itself most readily to your purposes. This in turn will depend upon the area in which you choose to buy (see Chapter 1). Additionally, the cost of works must be taken into account, and the time which will be needed to complete them and sell, for this will dictate exactly the outgoings which you must allow for interest payments on loans.

Once your research tour of estate agents' offices has yielded an approximate rock-bottom purchase price for the type of premises you want to buy, you will have the basis for the drawing up of an overall budget.

You must work out a costing comprising all the main items of expenditure on the kind of project you propose to tackle at this stage. These are:

The purchase money
The cost of the works
Fees to solicitors, estate agents, surveyors and architects
Interest on loans.

More about these shortly, but where do you start with all these calculations? It may seem as if we're suggesting that you have to pull these figures out of thin air.

The method is fairly straightforward: once you have familiarised youself with the types of property available in your proposed area of purchase, and before you get involved in making offers or having surveys carried out, or any other of the preparations for a specific purchase, select *one* house which is as typical as possible of the kind you want for the first project—a good example would be a smallish Victorian property with three floors which might convert into three flats (one storey each) or one flat and one maisonette (two storeys). By deciding on a particular property you will be able to use it to make up a general blueprint which could be applied to any one of a number of houses which you may have your eye on. This is much more practical than wasting time estimating exact costs on one specific house which might be sold to someone else before you could buy it yourself.

You must, in any event, have a budget and plan of campaign drawn up *before* buying the property, otherwise you run the risk of being lumbered with a white elephant; the final selling price of the finished product of your work—the renovated house or the newly-built flats—also enters into this, for it is the true financial return on your efforts. It is on the prevailing local prices for homes comparable in size and facilities to those which you will be offering for sale which this figure will depend.

To summarise the above, the following are the parameters to decide if a particular house is a suitable purchase for renovation (or conversion):

1. *What is the lowest price you can buy for?*
The best bet first time round is a small property suitable for conversion into two or three units.

2. *How much will the work cost?*

3. *How much will you have to pay in fees to:*
   (a) Solicitors (for negotiating the purchase and resale and conveyancing the property—see Chapter 6).
   (b) Estate agents (for selling the property if you cannot sell it by other means).
   (c) Surveyors (for surveying the property purchased and possibly others which the surveys proved unsuitable).
   (d) Architects for drawing up plans, and obtaining planning permission. (If you are not prepared to do this yourself).
   (e) Stamp duty, at 1 per cent of the total value on property bought for over £30,000. A house bought for £20,000 attracts no stamp duty; one bought for £30,100 will attract £301.

Remember that (a), (c) and (d) might be involved on more than one property—ie, failed attempts to purchase.

4. *How much interest will you have to pay on loans,* ie, how long will it take to complete the work *and sell* the property?

Also, does a partner expect a minimum return on his capital? If so add it to this figure.

5. *How much can you* realistically *expect to sell for?*
To get the answer, subtract 1, 2, 3, and 4 from 5.

The figure left is your profit. Is it enough for you, bearing in mind the amount of your time which the project will take up?

If there is *no* profit to be had on the basis of your calculations with the above system, the project may still be worth doing if you intend to undertake a considerable part of the work yourself, as you will pay yourself a wage out of category 2, the funds allocated to the work.

Above all, you must allow a reasonable amount of leeway in 5 for the house to stand on the market unsold for some time, particularly if it will not be completed in the spring or early summer, which is when most purchases are made. Even properties with everything going for them can be quirky in this respect.

If the property you intend to purchase passes these tests with flying colours then you are in business in no uncertain terms!

Change of use and planning permission
Some properties on the market may already have permission from the local authority for a 'change of use', and planning permission for conversion into flats. This will probably have been obtained by the vendor to make selling easier, or maybe he had intended to convert himself and changed his mind. If you decide to buy one of these houses there need be no delays to prevent you starting work once you are the owner.

Where this is not the case, the agent should be able to tell you if an application for permission stands a good chance of being well received by the council or corporation. This usually depends on housing policy for the area. Some areas are kept strictly to single-dwelling properties. Houses in others where there has already been a degree of 'multiple occupation', ie, conversion of single dwellings into flats, are generally allowed to be divided up. They are granted change of use as a matter of course.

In any event, whatever the agent says, if you are very interested in the property, contact your local authority to find out from the horse's mouth if they are likely, not only to grant change of use, but more specifically agree to the kind of layout which you propose to feature in the property. It is worth checking with the Development Control Officer whether planning permission for conversion into flats is dependent on the developer's ability to provide car parking space for each of the new units. This varies according to the area. These minimal checks cover the risk of any error on the part of the agent. By this method you can find out as near as is humanly possible *before* you send in a formal request for planning permission whether it is likely to be accepted or not.

At this stage it is advisable not to trust *anyone* completely. Keep asking questions until you are satisfied either that plans exist and have formally been approved (ask the estate agent to show them to you and if doubtful get an architect to check if the layout is workable), or that the council is amenable to your intentions. At this stage comes the largest element of risk in the project: at some point you have to take a blind leap, and this is it.

Once as reassured as you can be on this score, you must acknowledge that to some extent the granting of these permissions is in the lap of the gods. It is very seldom practical to go any further with the matter at this stage of the proceedings; a formal submission for planning permission may require as many as eight or nine copies of detailed plans and proposals to be prepared and sent to the local authority for scrutiny. The whole process, from preparation of the plans through to the decision by the authority whether to give consent, can take three or four months, or even longer. All the more reason to check if the way seems clear *before* you start to apply formally, and especially *before* you buy the property. But, if you are as sure as you can be of the acceptability from the planning angle, and with your budget calculated, the house you have chosen is a good candidate for your renovation.

Properties not needing change of use or planning permission
If you decide to plump for renovating rather than converting into flats, and the house has been used as one dwelling only, it will not be subject to change of use or planning permission. This, of course, also applies to properties already in use as flats at the time of purchase (you may intend to revamp a house with this layout, and simply modernise and improve the existing flat units in it). However, there is less potential for profit with these types of scheme than with converting a house into flats, so it's six of one...

Assuming you have raised your funds by this stage, all that remains to be done is to go ahead with the standard procedures which anyone buying property is subject to. These are:

- Having the property surveyed
- Having the property conveyanced

● Making an offer in order to purchase the property.

These items are dealt with in Chapter 4.

Planning permission: some details of the procedure

The place to contact is the Planning Department of the local authority; ask what is needed.

Change of use
If converting from house to flats, this is relatively simple: the answer is 'yes' or 'no'. If the answer is 'yes':

Submit the application for planning permission
This will consist of architect's drawings of the new layout, showing plan views of each floor of the building, and elevation views of any relevant external aspects (front and rear of the property, and the sides if altered), and in some cases a plan view of the roof layout.

Items shown should be:

(a) Structural alterations, eg opened-up walls, with details of arrangements for supporting the weight of the structure over the new opening, ie rolled steel joists etc.

(b) New plumbing, drainage over and below ground, ventilation, insulation, sizes of new doors and windows.

Your local authority planning department will farm out copies of the plans to various departments (you will have to supply them with sufficient numbers). These will include copies to:

The District Surveyor (DS), or Borough Surveyor, or Building Inspector. He will deal with (a) above, and will be interested in lintel sizes, wall loadings and specifications for concrete mixes. He will also be the official who comes to see if the property conforms with the fire regulations when the work is done. (The 'DS', as he is called, is also a very helpful informal source of advice on site during the job, for his experience has made him aware of the difficulties involved in translating drawings into reality.)

The Environmental Health Officer. He will check that the items in (b) are acceptable.

The Grants Officer (usually, in practice, a Health Officer). Sometimes you will have to ask specifically if the proposals are eligible for a grant, sometimes you will be told as a matter of course.

Other departments, eg Historic Buildings. If the building has been classified by this department as being of historic interest, there may be restrictions upon what you can do to it. These apply mainly to the exterior of the property.

The planning permission saga can be a long and tedious business. The only way you can sidestep it with no risk is if you are just carrying out a straightforward refurbishing job on a single dwelling. Even so, you will be obliged to send details of structural alterations to the DS and plans of any but the most minor changes in drainage to the Health Officer.

Once over this hurdle, it's a relief to find that the people behind these titles are very often easy to work with and not lacking a sense of humour; there are, of course, exceptions...

It is possible to prepare the plans yourself if you are so inclined. Try to familiarise yourself with the conventions and symbols used by architects in plans and written specifications of works which often accompany them (the Penguin *Dictionary of Building* is useful here). While drawing plans you can also mark in the positions of electrical points, lights and switches, radiators and gas fires, consumer units (or fuse boxes), and gas and electricity mains and meters. None of these need be shown for local authority purposes, but they are of tremendous assistance in planning and carrying out the work.

Chapter 4
Buying the Property

Once you have decided that the house is a viable proposition for your purposes and have satisfied yourself by carrying out preliminary enquiries as outlined in Chapter 3, you should put in an offer on the most suitable property available. You are still relatively uncommitted to anything at this stage.

The sequence of events

Make your offer:

1. *Subject to contract,* and
2. *Subject to survey.*

Number 1 keeps you off the hook until the vendor starts getting serious and the drafting of contracts takes place, at which point it starts getting progressively more difficult (though by no means impossible) to back out of the deal.

Number 2 protects you against having to break your neck rushing around organising surveys on every property you may be keen enough on to make a potentially binding offer for, or at least cause bad feeling in the vendor's camp if you backed out.

You are not obliged to have a survey carried out at all. You must choose, depending on whether you have any knowledge of building construction and, if so, how much, between several alternatives.

(a) An all-the-stops-out survey, costing possibly £200 or more, will tell you far more than anyone would ever want to know about the building.

   The overly pessimistic tone of these documents would be enough to convince the uninitiated that no house is ever fit to be lived in, but with this kind you are paying for the fine-tooth comb approach, and that's what you get.

(b) The other extreme is to cast a weather eye over the edifice and draw your own conclusions. Of course this is all right only if you have considerable experience.

But if you don't want to kiss goodbye to the sort of money needed for an extensive survey, there is now a 'mini-survey' at a fraction of the cost, which will tell you all you need to know about potential weak points, hazards, and shortcomings in the structure itself without telling you if there is a draught under the kitchen door and so on.

If the survey comes out well, whatever form it takes, you next need to have the local authority search carried out. This is a check on the legalities connected with the property in the same way as the survey is a check on its structural soundness. You can make your offer:

3. *Subject to search,* in the same way as you made it subject to factors 1 and 2. At this stage, the only tangible form of commitment to the property you will have to make is to fork out a:

4. *Stakeholder's deposit.* This is a nominal sum which shows willing and reinforces the 'gentlemen's agreement' which is still all that exists between you and the vendor to prove that your interest in the property is genuine and not just an offbeat way of passing the time. Once

5. *The survey* (or similar) has been carried out, if you are still interested in the property and

6. *The offer is accepted*

7. *The local authority search* must be commenced. This is where your solicitor really gets to work. Up till now the only involvement he may have had with the transaction will have been in the formal confirmation of the offer with the vendor's solicitor. The survey is your responsibility, but he will now commence the checks on the status of the property. This involves:

(a) Checking there are no compulsory purchase orders on the property—your house could be in the path of a proposed new motorway, and as such capable of being forcibly 'purchased' from you by the local authority at a fraction of its true value.
(b) Ensuring that there is no order for demolition or expensive repairs imposed by the Environmental Health Department. Either would cost you dearly.
(c) Checking the deeds of the property. They will show if the person you have offered to buy from is really the owner of the property. They will also show boundary demarcations with adjacent properties etc.

All of these checks come under the general title of:

8. *Conveyancing.* You can do this yourself if you wish (see reading list on page 137) but a good solicitor will take care of it all and you need then only involve yourself when he refers to you details which he thinks you should know about.

If all is well you can press on to the next stage:

9. *Drawing up the contracts.* You and the vendor each have a contract drawn up for you by your own solicitor. These are then exchanged and signed by the other party (still supervised by the solicitors).

10. *Exchange of contracts* has then taken place, and this is the stage at which you start parting with bigger funds—usually 10 per cent of the purchase price of your house.

Within a statutory time limit, usually around four weeks,

11. *Completion* must take place. At this stage the transaction is complete; the keys are handed over to you and the remaining 90 per cent (minus shareholder's deposit) is paid to the vendor. You are now:

12. *The new owner.*

Sources of properties

1. Estate agents
In discussing the typical sequence of events in a purchase, the above example deals with a property advertised through an estate agent. The premises would have been offered for sale at a fixed rate, around which offers would be based. Although you may have got to know more about property generally by your 'tour' of their offices (see Chapter 3) you do not necessarily have to buy from an estate agent.

2. Private purchase
If you should get to hear through the grapevine that a house is being put up for sale, you can contact the vendor and buy from him directly. This cuts out the expense of the estate agent's fee (usually 2 to 3 per cent of the purchase price). As you will have saved the vendor this expense, you can ask him to reduce his price a little accordingly.

3. Auctions

Usually conducted by estate agents, auctions *can* be a useful means of buying. You will have to look extremely carefully for bargains if you attempt to purchase this way.

Properties offered for sale by auction are usually in such rough condition that it is impossible to get a building society mortgage for them, hence they are seldom offered at a fixed price in the agent's office window because they will be taking up valuable space which could be used for more saleable properties. They are only viable propositions for builders, renovators and others who can raise ready cash to buy them and devote considerable time, effort and resources to refurbishing.

There are bargains to be had here, but be careful. It's easy to get carried away in the excitement of the auction room, and the longer the bidding goes on the more it seems the house must be worth. Here are a few tips on how to proceed:

(a) *The auction programme.* This is available from the estate agent or auctioneer some time before the auction. Get a copy. If there are any properties which interest you, quiz the agent about them at this stage while you still have enough time to sort yourself out. The last few precious days before the auction will slip away like seconds.

(b) *Maximum bid for each property.* You must try to estimate the costs involved on each potential purchase, ie buying, converting, etc. Fix a cut-off point for each house on which you propose to bid—your maximum offer. This may be a different figure for different properties, as some will be larger than others and will require more work, even though they will eventually bring a greater return on resale. Others may be more expensive but need less work done, thus involving the same total outlay.

Profitability of the project is the bottom line, remember, so once the bidding has reached your cut-off point, drop out or face unpleasant consequences later.

(c) *Securing a purchase in the auction room.* If your bid is accepted, things start to happen much faster in the auction room than in a transaction through an estate agent. The contract of sale is drawn up on the back of the auction catalogue and you will be required to put pen to paper at this stage, which is equivalent to exchange of contracts in the other method of purchase.

You will almost certainly be expected to hand over 10 per

cent of the purchase money in ready cash at this stage. (This brings back fond memories of sitting with £4000 in one's pocket for a whole afternoon!) The balance of payment must usually be made within a set period from the date of the auction. This is about two weeks as a rule.

As with the other kind of purchase—see 1—if you do not pay the balance within this period you may forfeit your deposit, although if the vendor's camp feels that there are unavoidable delays and that the money will eventually be forthcoming, this 'completion date' can be extended.

4. Sealed bids

Sometimes a different form of bidding is used: each bidder writes down one bid—the highest he thinks he will need to outbid the opposition—and seals it in an envelope. The bidders are called to a special meeting by the auctioneer, at which the bids are opened in full view. The highest bid secures the property.

The most obvious feature about this kind of sale is that each bidder is completely in the dark about how much his competitors have bid. This has both a good and a bad side; there is no risk of bidding more than you intend in the heat of the moment, which could happen in the auction room, but as you only have one shot you must take care not to bid too low. Where sealed bidding is used you will be told the reserve price—the minimum figure the vendor is prepared to sell for—by the estate agent beforehand. (If only two or three bidders are involved, all concerned will not want to waste time on the exercise because everyone has put in too low a bid to effect a purchase.)

Often sealed bidding is used for properties which have been withdrawn from open auction after failing to reach their reserve price. This means that if you were at the open auction you will have had a chance to check out the opposition during the bidding there. This can be followed up by a chat to the estate agent where you may get more clues as to your chances of successfully clinching a sale.

Summary of methods of purchase

1. By far the commonest form of house purchase is through estate agents by means of an offer made to the vendor via the agent. The property will be on the agent's books at a set asking price.

Remember—you do not have to offer the asking price. Even

with the cheapest premises you should make an offer which is at least £2000 lower, or thereabouts. This is irrespective of other factors such as a grossly unrealistic asking price, or any features which make it seem a gift. The vendor will almost certainly be asking more than he expects to get—it's one of the silly money games in the property business, but you have to go along with it.

2. The private purchase—the best if you can find one.

3. The auction—more tricky than the other two types. It's not a good idea to attempt an auction purchase for your first project.

Chapter 5
Unusual Buildings

There is a wide range of building types available for renovation
and conversion. Some of these will already have been in use as
homes, while others can be adapted for this purpose. With a little
imagination almost any building can be modified for use as a dwelling, planning authorities willing.

There are many special advantages in this kind of project: conversions of more exotic and even outlandish buildings, from old
schoolhouses and mills to barns and lighthouses, attract more
potential buyers than your average semi-detached or terraced
property, merely by virtue of their curiosity value; the prospect of
living in a 'different' sort of home sets off most people's imagination on a flight of fancy which may end in the signing of a large
cheque!

Special interest

Working on less run-of-the-mill types of building has its own
rewards, quite apart from the profit angle: unusual shapes—a
hexagonal turnpike cottage on an old toll road; a series of round
rooms one above the other in a windmill; large, high-ceilinged
rooms with galleries around the walls in a chapel, with possibly an
underground tunnel leading to a nearby cellar—all these eccentri-
cities can make a pleasant change of workplace, and a fascinating
challenge for restoration and adaptation.

Unusual room shapes and layouts can stimulate unusual solutions to the problems of where to put new doors, partitions, bathrooms etc. When the process of conversion is complete, all this can
make the interior of a building even more intriguing than it was
originally. For instance, many examples of a classic piece of
English vernacular architecture, the Kentish barn, are supported
by an elaborate and, although primitive, ornate framework of
wooden beams hewn largely by hand with the adze rather than
sawn and planed. With care this striking feature can be integrated

into any new partition walls erected within the shell of the building to form flats or smaller rooms, giving a raised textured motif of rough-hewn, sinewy woodwork set in smooth white plaster. Such a feature would be difficult to devise from scratch, with its apparently random deviations from the rules of symmetry and rectangularity.

Another example of a building with this freedom of skeletal form is the cruck house, the structure of which is supported around a frame based on two inverted v-shaped wishbone-style timbers. The cruck house also benefits from the white plaster treatment described above.

Many of these older buildings will have their own unique features — hand-pump for water, an open 'wishing well', a working or repairable water-wheel, a trout stream running through the grounds. Once out of town, the renovator can choose to work on properties which offer sea views, rolling countryside and tranquillity as key items for the estate agent's pamphlet.

The sight of an old building may be deceptive however: many near-ruins exude an atmosphere of history and romance, but putting them into good order may mean virtual demolition first. Rebuilding from scratch could be the only practical way to cure rising damp in buildings with no dampcourse, the only means of eliminating rot, the only economic way to make the structure strong enough to provide living accommodation on additional storeys. A seventeenth-century barn may have provided adequate shelter for generations of dairy cattle, but the regulation standards of weatherproofing required for human habitation may be beyond the reach of a quick revamp.

This poses a major problem which many renovators end up learning about the hard way: rebuilding from scratch inevitably results in a loss of some of the character of an old building. Wooden weatherboarding and siding to old barns and cottages, which has subtly taken on a life of its own, twisting, warping and turning a mellow shade of brown over the centuries, can at present only be replaced with timber sawn and planed by machine, which comes from the sawmill cut straight as a die. Old hand-made clay roof tiles, made on site while the lower sections of a building were being assembled, each of a slightly different shape and colour, have no acceptable modern equivalent; tiles are now machine-cut before firing, and identical in size, shape and colour. Famous types of brick like the yellow or mixed London Stock, once hand-made and with a textured surface, slightly different from each other in contour and shading, now have a homogeneous appearance thanks to mass-production methods.

This loss of the continuous and visually stimulating variation in contour and colour has been one of the crucial factors in the increasingly uninteresting aspect of more contemporary structures.

While the most able and aware renovators and builders appreciate the subtleties involved in the use of old and new materials and artefacts, insisting on using original items wherever possible, these are often in short supply and a modern equivalent must be used. At worst the need to rebuild from scratch can mean that all you are really buying when you put down a deposit on that Tudor cottage with 'potential' is the *idea* of having such a building on this particular site, and the sanction of the local authority to build it again pretty much as it was. In cold hard fiscal terms this means that while you may need to spend no money applying for planning permission to rebuild it, you *will* have to pay for the demolition of this dream home. Whether its replacement captures that elusive essential charm which attracted your interest in the first place will be very much down to the skills of the architect, builder or craftsman engaged to perform the task. These skills are not yet as common as we might wish.

On the brighter side, the general move towards a greater appreciation of the traditional crafts and skills in the building world is encouraging the rise of many small firms offering services and products which once seemed destined to disappear for good. Handmade tiles, terracotta pottery, specialised painting and decorating techniques all represent a trend which can only grow. In the meantime it's worth bearing in mind that even a rebuilt oast house or Kentish barn *can* look as dull as a high-rise block of flats.

To summarise, do a double take the first time you cast eyes on that centuries-old dream home: it can be restored to an identical appearance, but you must take care.

Different types of unusual buildings

Here is a list of a few possibilities, with some brief notes on good and bad points.

Cottages
The prettier ones in country areas will be instantly appealing to a wide range of potential buyers, or highly suitable for holiday letting.

However beautiful the roses round the door, and the surrounding countryside, small cracks in the walls may indicate serious settlement and land subsidence problems, ie the building probably has no foundations, or footings, under the walls. The only solution to this problem is painstaking underpinning and rebuilding. This entails digging a trench up to 1 metre deep under all walls, and filling with concrete, followed by rebuilding damaged brickwork or stonework. New work is often difficult to match with old and can look unsightly.

One cottage in Sussex which we looked at had everything going for it—a traditional English garden in full bloom, wooden verandahs, perfect proportions, spacious grounds—except that it was sliding down a gentle slope towards the nearby road, having no footings to the walls and a deep cellar which aggravated the problem of small but lethal cracks in the brickwork.

Summary
Plenty of good buys are available, especially suitable for renovation and resale or letting, in up-and-coming areas where prices are still low, such as Yorkshire and Norfolk. These are normally within the price range of many wanting a change from a terraced or semi-detached dwelling in the towns and cities, as a main or second home.

Barns
With many barns you have a clean slate for your own ideas. Most of them consist of only one or two huge open rooms which can be subdivided or merely refurbished as one large open living space, New York loft style. Surprisingly, many barns are *very* large indeed—a glance in *Country Life* will usually reveal a couple of examples of barn conversions for sale which may be of the order of up to 200 feet long and 30 or 40 feet wide. Such properties, while not a good idea as a first restoration project, provide an opportunity not only to create several separate dwellings and recoup some of your outlay with ease as you proceed, but also to create a pleasant surrounding environment. Tidying up the nearby duck-pond (or putting one in), laying a curved gravel drive, and generally enhancing the atmosphere of the location by sympathetic remodelling of the substantial grounds which usually accompany such properties can reap great benefits.

In many cases barns in need of restoration are offered by estate agents as 'kits', as it were, with planning permission already granted on plans already submitted by an architect. Such kits will have been fully costed so that the overall outlay including building work is a known quantity from the start. The builder may even be ready and waiting on the sidelines to start work as per his already supplied quotation. Such deals are particularly common in the South East, especially in Kent.

The remarks under Cottages above about inadequate foundations and rot problems apply here. There may be difficulties in getting planning permission, too.

Summary
An interesting proposition with plenty of scope for imaginative restyling, but better tackled as a later rather than a first-time venture.

Mills
Every imaginable variety of building, from small single rooms to large rambling complexes. Many windmills are now used as homes, and the best examples have been restored complete with a full set of sails. Watermills have the additional attraction of scenic stretches of water, while windmills, being tall to catch the wind, usually afford good views of the surrounding landscape from their upper storeys. In addition to providing living accommodation, many renovators also restore the mechanisms of windmills and watermills to full working order (some even mill flour on a commercial basis as the demand for traditionally produced foods gathers momentum). In isolated locations wind and water mills can provide their own electric power via generators connected to the sails or waterwheel.

A good example of a watermill in full commercial use is to be found in Dunster, North Devon. Visitors can walk around, see the various stages of milling and follow the water as it works its way through the mill, providing power for the mechanical processes involved. A visit to such a project will give the would-be renovator useful ideas for his own efforts, and help to get the creative juices going.

The restoration of most derelict mills is a major undertaking, and should only be tackled by the experienced builder or renovator, or those of you with more than your fair share of the pioneering spirit and more than a dash of insanity. A glance around any working or intact windmill will reveal not only the complexity but the sheer weight of the mechanism. The cap alone of the tower-type mill can weigh around 20 tons. This top section, which rotates by running on wheels in a circular track around the top of the brick wall of the mill, carries the weight of the sail and windshaft assembly. A windmill is a mass of heavy machinery, much of it consisting of gear wheels and shaft hand-crafted from fruitwoods — fascinating and challenging, but time-consuming to rebuild. However, there is a vast reservoir of information in the literature both on the general architecture of mills and the craftsmanship and specific skills required to rebuild them (see reading list).

Summary
Mills are a challenge, but mug up on your background reading before you take one on, and be prepared to end up spending at least four times as much money and time on your new project as you had originally planned. The variety of types caters for all tastes. In addition to the more familiar brick or stone-built tower mill, with its characteristic round floor plan and domed revolving cap, there are also the less common but still extant smock mills and post mills. These are rarer because of their shorter-lived wooden construction, but possibly even more elegant.

Churches and chapels
Many interesting and varied properties are available. The large number of conversions already carried out provide a good range of ideas for the would-be developer. Many conversions of churches have show flats which will yield some useful ideas. Churches offer scope for unique and striking features — stained glass windows, ornate carved woodwork, high ceilings and imposing stonework. Some of the more outlying chapels in the country areas — the West Country for instance — are built with walls of cob (mud and horsehair with stones) and have galleries and staircases rough-hewn with the adze.

Cob buildings can be difficult to repair. Church conversion requires very specialised building skills.

Summary
Conversions of ecclesiastic buildings are now fairly common compared with a few years ago, and there is a continuous flow of them on to the market. There are many companies which specialise in this sort of work, and there is always a ready market for living accommodation which is a little out of the ordinary.

Oast houses

The oast houses of Kent, with their striking pointed roof-mounted cowls, are a natural choice for anyone who wants a distinctive-looking home. Apart from the familiar cowl, another feature of many of these buildings is their size—some may be as large as 200 feet by 50 or so, though it is possible to find the odd one which is only 20 feet square: hence they may be used for multiple or single accommodation. But there aren't many left!

Summary
Difficult to find, but easily saleable or rentable after reconstruction.

Schools

Good examples of Victorian architecture at its best, showing many small-scale tours de force—fancy brickwork, chimneys, tiling etc. These are also getting a little thin on the ground.

Summary
Tall, galleried rooms can make a nice feature in converted schools. Windows are often high, but this gives privacy and plenty of natural light.

Railway stations, signal boxes and other railside buildings

A wide range of choices—large, small, isolated, in town centres and on disused lines as well as ones currently in use. The main disadvantage is the proximity, in some cases, of fast trains and noise.

Summary
Chance of a deal with British Rail to commute from your doorstep.

Toll-houses

Interesting shaped buildings, often with splendid folly-style decor in the form of elaborate chimneys, gates etc. But they are always at the roadside and hence in many cases near continuous traffic.

Summary
The looks alone will sell these places.

Gatekeepers' cottages on country estates etc

These buildings were usually show-pieces, the first evidence of the landowner's wealth which visitors to his estate would clap eyes on as they drew up to the gates. Many are of modest size which helps to keep the cost down despite the decor, but they are often near busy roads.

Summary
As for toll-houses.

Castles
The further north you go, the cheaper they get: prices may start as low as £100,000 for a small specimen in a deserted location. An excellent prospect for conversion into multiple units on the grand scale. Massive grounds, and becoming increasingly popular with developers. Pleasant locations, many with exclusive hunting and fishing rights.

Very, very expensive to renovate and maintain (multiply the purchase cost by five at least to cover alterations and repairs). Essentially a top end of the market area.

Summary
A good bet to set up as timeshare projects—collective purchase for short holiday purposes by a group of 20 or more buyers, but requiring an awesome level of commitment in time, money and sheer bravery!

Mews properties
Although rarely for sale, and invariably pricey, there are some interesting specimens around, and sometimes a little one comes on to the market. The television programme *On the House* in March 1988 featured the purchase and improvement of a small mews dwelling; the woman who bought it in tatty condition had been walking past it for years on her way to and from work, and decided to take the plunge and buy when she saw the 'for sale' sign outside.

Consisting of just one room 17 feet by 12 plus a small toilet and alleyway garden, it received the interior designer treatment for better or for worse. It benefited from the addition of a raised clerestory-style roof with sidelights, giving natural but indirect light from above in addition to the wall window, installation of a 5 foot square kitchen with cooking hob, microwave and small dishwasher, *trompe l'oeil* garden, new bay window and window seat. The lady concerned was well satisfied. Cost? Initial purchase price £56,000, cost of works £31,000, subsequent market value when completed £150,000.

'Bijou' properties, invariably with lashings of character, easy resale, good potential profit margain.

Cramped access for workers and materials, small space to work in, parking restrictions, likelihood of friction with neighbours during the renovations owing to the restricted space. Limited opportunities for obtaining such properties.

Summary
Worth looking for.

Other
This includes the ultimate follies such as Martello towers (built to act as lookout posts for advance warning of Napoleon's possible invasion from the English Channel), sea forts, lighthouses, and houseboats, not to mention wooden sheds in the middle of fields!

Projects like this provide a safety-valve for the slightly loony. And there's a ready market for them. In March 1988 one of the aforementioned sheds, in unrestored state, was for sale near Westerham in Kent. It was derelict. It stood in half an acre of land, in a jungle of weeds, half a mile from the nearest road. Measuring just 10 feet by 8, with peeling wallpaper and rotten timberwork, it was described by the agents as a 'desirable and interesting detached dwelling of timber construction'(!) and offered for sale at £30,000. The venerable construction attracted 80 enquiries on its first day on the market, and was soon sold for £55,000. Clearly the peace and quiet of the countryside and the attractions of a little plot of land continue to exert their charm.

Preserving period features
Having gone to great lengths to buy something a little offbeat, it's worth taking some trouble not only to reinstate damaged parts of the building but also to ensure that any new windows, doors, extensions and fittings preserve the feel of the building's period and the style of the craftsmen who worked on it. Much of this may be common sense, but it's also common sense to get advice from local builders and architects, or perhaps the original owner's family, as well as reading a little about the styles and practices of the time the building was constructed.

While expense can often seem to be a good reason for cutting a few corners, just as often a little thought and a few enquiries may provide a cheaper solution which is at the same time more architecturally appropriate. Hugh Lander's books offer excellent practical tips on how to renovate tastefully (see reading list).

Capitalising on the unusual features of a building

The curiosity value of unusual buildings is a useful factor both for selling and for letting, and it makes sense not merely to let the architecture speak for itself but also to furnish a few details of its history: every exotic building has an interesting past, and investigation will usually prove there are plenty of equally exotic locals on hand to tell you about it.

Why not compile a handbook outlining the story of the building, not least the saga of your renovation project? Many properties let as holiday homes have a journal which describes the renovation — its progress, triumphs and setbacks, how it was planned and carried out — and a logbook for visitors to write their observations about the property and its environs, the locals, and what they think of their stay in the area. This adds interest to any holiday, and the number of entries in these logs shows how it captures people's imagination. Any self-respecting historic building, however modest, can benefit by having its own journal, whether it is to be let or sold.

If you decide to let a property, a few photographs taken at various stages of its career can work wonders in capturing the imagination of your tenants. Anthony Triggs' *The Windmills of Hampshire* shows Langstone Mill, on the shore of Langstone Harbour, built in 1730, in various stages of repair and disrepair. There are six illustrations, one of them an engraving showing the mill in full sail. But by far the most striking is a photograph of the building virtually surrounded by pack ice in the great freeze of 1895 — and this was a *windmill*! Such photographs also help to remind people of the value of maintaining old buildings in good order for their own sake. Illustrations also help your property to stick in people's memories, and they will be more likely to recommend it to their friends.

Researching the renovation

There are many organisations offering every kind of property for holiday letting, but some specialise in the more exotic. For instance, the Landmark Trust rent out anything from Welsh mountain cottages with access only by a mile of footpath to the splendidly named Fort Clonque in the Channel Islands, which is a vestige of wartime sea defences. A few short stays at some of their faraway places will be an education in what can be accomplished with willpower and dedication on the part of the renovator.

This organisation operates along the same lines as the National

Trust except that it concerns itself with the preservation and repair of old buildings rather than the countryside. It is non profit-making, essentially a charity, and ploughs all income from lettings back into repair work and the purchase of more properties. The Trust employs a band of workers both nationwide and locally based, who personify the pioneering spirit and are actively engaged in the tasteful restoration of many old, and some very peculiar, buildings. They are also more than willing to part with their often hard-won knowledge, and as such are a limitless fund of specialist experience on how to tackle these projects. Here is a perfect opportunity to combine research on how to renovate with a holiday in an unusual setting—the Landmark Handbook gives details of all properties which the organisation has available to let. A copy can be obtained from the Landmark Trust, Shottesbrooke, Maidenhead, Berkshire; 0628 82 3431.

Letting as an alternative to resale

This will have a particular attraction if you find a building you get so attached to that you can't face selling it once renovation is completed. Letting is unlikely to make a profit—at best eight months in the year is the maximum period most owners achieve—and wear and tear, letting agents' fees and setting aside time for one's own holidays all eat into the profits. However, it will enable the property to pay for itself—costs of repairs etc. Letting can be an extremely demanding and frustating business, but it can also be enlightening and rewarding. Most of this reward is non-financial, however, except with the largest properties, where time-share schemes and the like may be employed to great economic effect.

Chapter 6
Two Typical Projects

In this chapter we have taken examples of two types of property commonly encountered during the course of renovation work. The profits can, of course, be greater than indicated in areas affected by rapid house price inflation.

The first is a house suitable for conversion into two flats. It is a medium-sized three-storey property converting into a one-bedroom basement flat and a two-bedroom maisonette.

As explained in Chapter 1, the property must be suitable for conversion without too much alteration. Ideally, it should have two separate entrances (one for each proposed flat); say, for example, a main front door to the ground floor and a side entrance to the basement. This arrangement means that you have only to remove the staircase to the basement and seal off the resulting gap to make the basic separation into two units, and it will have been achieved without a lot of structural work.

Converting into two flats means, of course, that you will have to install two of everything—kitchens, bathrooms, gas meters, water tanks, and so on—and when you sell, two lots of solicitor's fees. You will also need planning permission because you intend to 'change the use' of the property. However, having said that, the profits are nearly always higher when converting property into flats, and this type of property is ideal for a first conversion.

Conversion of a three-storey house into two flats

Here is a typical breakdown of the work involved in this conversion:

	£
Purchase of property	65,000
Fees etc (solicitors, stamp duty, telephone, District Surveyor, excluding estate agent)	1,400
Separation into two units	700
Two bathrooms	2,500

	£
Two kitchens	2,800
Two electrical installations	2,300
Extension to basement flat	2,500
Roof work	1,200
Plastering/external render	800
Damp-proof course	800
Drainage/plumbing	1,200
Gas supplies	200
Two central heating installations	3,200
Painting/decorating	1,400
Carpentry	1,000
Scaffolding	700
Garden	600
Contingencies	1,500
Total expenditure	89,800
Profit	35,200
Sale of two flats	125,000

The second example is a small three-storey house, unsuitable for conversion into flats (due to its size), but ideal for renovation as a two-bedroom family town house.

The criteria for selecting this type of property have already been discussed, so we won't go into them again except to say that planning permission for 'change of use' will not normally be required as you will not be changing the way in which the house was designed to be used.

Renovation will usually be cheaper and quicker than conversion, but again, profits could be lower and your prospective buyers will be more particular.

Renovation of a house as a single dwelling

Here is a typical breakdown of the work involved in this renovation:

	£
Purchase of property	90,000
Fees etc (solicitors, stamp duty, telephone, District Surveyor, excluding estate agent)	1,700
Bathroom	1,500
Kitchen	2,400

	£
Electrical installation	1,800
Roof work	1,800
Plastering/external render	3,200
Damp-proof course	1,000
Drainage/plumbing	1,800
Gas supply	400
Central heating	2,500
Painting/decorating	2,000
Carpentry	2,000
Scaffolding	1,000
Garden, rubbish clearance	900
Contingencies	1,700
Total expenditure	115,700
Profit	29,800
Sale of property	145,500

As can be seen, most of the items are the same in both examples, except that in the conversion into flats it was necessary to build a single-storey extension on to the basement flat to provide a bathroom. Even though building an extension can be an expensive item, the greater profit to be made from the sale of two flats (as opposed to one house) makes it easily affordable.

It will obviously take longer to do the conversion project than it will the renovation and any borrowed money will be tied up for longer. So the quicker and more efficient you are, the bigger will be your profits.

When designing your layout for a conversion into flats, try to keep as many of the services as possible confined to each flat. In other words, as an example, put separate cold water tanks in each flat rather than putting them all in the main loft. This will avoid the problem of residents having to go through each other's flats when they want to maintain or service their systems. It also makes installation cheaper because pipe work does not have to be run so far.

The same applies to electrical work. Try and keep consumer units (fuse boxes) within the relevant flat, rather than bunching them all together in a hall cupboard.

Separating items like this will ensure that each flat is properly self-contained, something which prospective buyers will appreciate.

Chapter 7
Professional Advice

Once you embark on a project of this nature, it is worth getting all the advice you can. If you know anyone who has done some work on their own home, even if what they have done seems trivial in comparison to the size of the project you intend to undertake, the knowledge they have gained will be valuable to you. It is often the small details and less important items that tend to get overlooked when tackling a large job.

Banks

Whether or not you are raising money from the bank, your bank manager is an excellent source of down-to-earth advice on money matters and business schemes generally. If you do intend to borrow from the bank, he will want to see details of your scheme, including:

- Total investment—yours and any other person's involved
- Cost of the property you intend to buy
- The total cost of renovation, including solicitors' and estate agents' fees, and bank interest
- A detailed breakdown of how the money will be spent, as described in the specimen sheet in Chapter 6
- How long the work will take (be realistic).

The more detail you present to your bank manager, the more impressed he will be with your organising ability, and the more detailed his advice will be. He may also want to have a look at the property you intend to buy.

Solicitors and accountants

Your solicitor, if you have chosen him carefully, will provide you with information on company law, conveyancing, auctions and legal requirements generally. His advice is not free, of course, but as you will undoubtedly have to consult him anyway, you might as well cover as much ground as you can in one visit.

Another invaluable source of professional advice is an accountant. As with solicitors, try to choose one who is used to dealing with small businesses and perhaps has some knowledge of property companies. He can advise on self-employment; company law (if you intend to form a company); your tax position in respect of income tax, capital gains tax, corporation tax and PAYE. It is absolutely essential to sort out your tax position and possible liabilities before you set up your business and start any actual work.

As your accountant will be the one who looks at what you have spent and how you have spent it on an annual basis, he will be able to offer advice from time to time on how you are shaping up as a property dealer.

Architects

At some point you will need drawings of your proposed renovation (for local authorities etc). Apart from supplying you with professional drawings, the architect will be in the position to offer advice on what he thinks will work in a practical sense in your property and, of course, what won't work. If he is used to designing layouts for domestic properties, he will be aware of the most detailed aspects of house renovation.

Free advice

There are plenty of sources of free professional advice. It may seem to you that you will become confused by taking advice from every possible quarter, but it is worthwhile taking it all in and then evaluating what is going to be useful now and what perhaps will help you later on.

The following are particularly useful:

● *Estate agents.* They can help enormously by advising on property values in a particular area. They can tell you what sort of price you should pay for the property you are considering and what sort of price you should expect to get after your renovation. They have their fingers right on the property pulse and can tell you which type of property (eg, flats or bed-sits) is more in demand, and will therefore sell quickly, in a particular area. They are keen to advise because you may be buying your property from them initially, and you may be selling the finished product through them. Their advice on how to set out your conversion (where to put kitchens, bathrooms etc) is also worth having. You can even get a cross-section of ideas from several agents.

● *Inland Revenue.* Your local tax office will supply you with booklets and leaflets on any taxes you are likely to encounter, and on PAYE, and on how to employ sub-contractors. You will need to approach them anyway if you intend to become self-employed.

● *VAT office* (listed in telephone directories under 'Customs and Excise'). They will supply you with information and booklets about what you can claim, should you be eligible for registration.

● *Insurance brokers.* They will advise on types of insurance that you will need in the course of buying and working on your property and, of course, will sell you the policies as well.

● *Local councils.* The town hall is a mine of information to someone renovating property. During the course of renovation you will become involved with the local authority departments, so it will be of benefit to you to go and see them before you start planning your first conversion/renovation, or making work schedules.

They will assess whether you are eligible for any grants and will advise on fire regulations, drainage, and anything else relevant to their interest in your property. In our experience they have always been extremely helpful.

● *Materials suppliers.* Visit large builders' merchants and specialised suppliers, and collect price-lists and information sheets on the products that you are likely to use. Also make notes of who sells what and whether materials are regularly in stock or have to be ordered. Check on whether suppliers will deliver reliably, as waiting for materials can cause irritating delays to your carefully planned work schedule.

The large builders' merchants can also advise on the suitability of particular materials, but whether or not you use them depends on whether there are good cheaper alternatives. It is up to you to check on prices and quality, as buying sensibly is crucial to making your expected profit on the finished job. Deciding whose advice to take isn't always easy. Generally, the more efficient the firm, the sounder the advice.

● *Other sources.* Friends who are architects or surveyors; friends who are builders and can offer practical advice; anyone you know who already runs his or her own business and can give advice on day-to-day running and control.

Chapter 8
Employing Others

In starting up a business of this nature from scratch it is unlikely that you will want to become involved in employing full-time staff. It would, in fact, be unwise to do so, because you will not be in a position to offer permanent, continuous employment by renovating one house at a time. Should you eventually progress to being able to buy and renovate several houses at the same time, it might be worth considering, but there are still drawbacks.

If you take on people as employees you will need to give them a contract of employment, provide sickness/accident and holiday pay, and pay employers' National Insurance contributions. You will also have to operate a PAYE tax scheme. Obviously, this would be time-consuming and expensive. So for this type of business it is much better to employ contractors and/or casual labour.

Contractors

A contractor can be a builder, who will carry out some or all of the work, or a specialist tradesman—electrician, plasterer, carpenter etc.

One advantage of using a contractor is that he will price the job (usually free of charge) for a fixed amount. This means that, barring a few possible extras, you will know before you start exactly what the work will cost. Another advantage of using contractors, rather than doing the work yourself, is that the quality of the work should be better. It will also get finished more quickly.

Having raised these points, it is necessary to say that there are good and bad contractors, and you should always try to use people who have been recommended, or who you have previously used yourself. If this is not possible, then try to look at some of the work they have done on other houses, and assess for yourself how good they are. Genuine builders and contractors won't mind you looking at examples of their work.

It is a good idea to get at least three quotes for any job you intend to contract out.

If you employ a builder to do most or all of the work, he then has the status of main contractor and it is quite likely that he will employ specialist trades himself. These specialists would then be sub-contractors to the builder and as such would be answerable only to him. Therefore, it is up to you to keep an eye on the quality and progress of work and take up problems as they arise with the builder himself.

Alternatively, you can act as the main contractor yourself, and bring in specialist trades as you need them.

The best way to get contractors to quote for a job is to supply them with drawings and a detailed specification. There is then no question of confusion over where things go and what should be done.

If you do intend to do the work yourself, you may employ help in the form of casual labour. Casual labour means exactly that. You employ people, generally unskilled, to work on your job a day or a week at a time without contract, and for an agreed labour figure only. This can be very useful, especially in the early stages of the job, when there is a lot of demolition and rubbish clearing to do. Also at the end of the job when there is clearing up, gardening and cleaning to do.

Supervision

Supervising the work as it proceeds is all-important in getting the results you want from the finished job. If you are going to run the site yourself you will be kept busy and you will have to be on your toes.

Once you have selected your contractors and accepted their quotes, you must arrange start dates. Try and keep to your programme (Chapter 9). Ask contractors for start dates in writing. They should be able to start within a few days of the date they give.

Try to arrange things so that there are not too many people working on the site at one time, especially if it is a small house. People get in each other's way and quality suffers. Also, if you are running things, it is important to establish who is buying materials and hiring plant/tools etc. If it is down to you, it is important to check on availability and delivery, and to get any materials on site before the work-force arrives, because they will want to start work immediately. If materials are not ready for them they will probably leave the site and you will then have to wait until it is convenient for them to fit you in again. An upset of this sort will then delay other contractors as well, so careful planning is very important.

If you are employing a builder to carry out all the work, then of course he will bring in sub-contractors at the appropriate time, and will probably want to supply materials as well. This will relieve you of a lot of planning and ordering, but is likely to cost you more, obviously.

Whether you run the site yourself or employ a builder, supervision by you is of paramount importance. You are the boss—it is your money that is being spent—and the people employed on the site are working for you. Don't get talked into taking short cuts just to make the builder's life easier. Do things the way you want to do them and in the way agreed in the quotes. This doesn't mean that there is no room at all for compromise. You will need a good working relationship with your builder, and you ought to be able to accept his advice on some matters, he probably having more practical experience than you.

If you are actually working on the site yourself then of course supervision is no problem; otherwise you should arrange a visit at least every other day (every day if you can manage it) to assess progress and sort out any problems that have arisen—and there will always be some. Contractors nearly always appreciate regular visits by their clients. Don't be afraid to point out things that are not to your liking. It is much easier to sort out problems as they occur, rather than when the whole job is finished.

When converting a house into flats, it is a good idea to try and finish one in advance of the others. This then acts as a show flat and you can put it on the market straight away. Should somebody be interested in buying, the deposit they put down could help your cash flow enormously.

Payment/Wages

Whether you form a company or partnership, or run the whole project on your own, you are treated as a contractor by the Inland Revenue.

This means that you are responsible for checking certain tax details before you employ people. If you employ contractors who are limited liability companies (they have the word 'Limited' after their name) or other corporate bodies, there is no special action required by you. Contractors who are not limited companies may or may not be holders of a tax exemption certificate. Those who are not, along with persons supplying casual labour, will involve you in more work. You will be required to deduct 25 per cent of all payments made to them up to £19,300, and 40 per cent thereafter (current rates), and to send those deducted payments regularly to the Inland Revenue. Your accountant can explain in detail.

Contractors who possess a current tax exemption certificate are required to show it to you, and you have to check that it is in order. You can then pay that contractor in full, without deduction of tax. The Inland Revenue issue pamphlets which explain the position in detail.

Once a contractor is on site (or even before) he will want some money. Most contractors ask for a deposit and then, depending on the length of the particular contract, further regular payments. These regular payments are known as stage payments because the money is paid in stages — weekly or monthly — in accordance with the amount of work done.

It is vital that you do not pay too much too soon. Assess the progress to date, with any extras, and agree a fair payment with the contractor bearing in mind that if he is supplying materials he will need more than someone supplying labour only.

Before making any final payment, make sure that everything has been done to the agreed specification, and that installations such as central heating, wiring etc actually work. It is in your own interest to make a list of any outstanding items, however small, and present it to the contractor before final payment.

Sometimes an agreement is made for retention of a portion of the contract sum for a set period, perhaps six months, to cover any faults that may occur, but this should be agreed before the contract is signed. Also make sure that guarantees are in order where applicable.

Casual employees are quite often paid daily in cash, but you must deduct tax and keep records.

Watching your renovation take shape is fascinating and rewarding, but the importance of supervision and site control cannot be over-stressed, nor can careful assessment of 'work done' before making payments.

Chapter 9
Running the Site

Settling down to your best method of working can take a little time, so it is best for you to spend some time on the site doing some of the preparatory work and generally getting the feel of working there. This familiarisation will help you when the major work starts to take place.

Daily operation

One of the first things to do is to produce a breakdown of the work to be undertaken. You should already have produced a schedule (page 72) and have a rough idea of the time each section of the work will take. By combining the two you can produce a programme for use on site which will give you easy reference to the state of progress on the site at any time. It will also help you to plan the arrival of contractors.

Try and arrange things so that one job leads on to the next. For example, laying new drainage and a new manhole would then allow the complete installation and testing of internal plumbing and sanitary ware. The sequence of operations is important and you should spend time working it out properly.

Fix your programme on a sheet of card and hang it on the wall where you can easily and quickly refer to it.

Even if you are doing all the work yourself, it is still worth having a programme.

You should also equip yourself with a site diary. Only by recording events daily can you run your project efficiently. It is often crucial to know, for example, when a contractor visited the site, or how many hours were worked on a particular day by someone you were paying by the hour. So record everything—it will pay dividends at the end of the job and will serve as an invaluable reference book on subsequent property conversions.

Site cleanliness
To make your site run well, it is necessary to keep it clean and tidy.

A daily sweep up keeps efficiency at a peak. Bag up rubbish as it accumulates and store it away from the working area. Arrange regular rubbish collections, or hire a skip.

Storage

A common problem, especially in a small house, is where to store materials. You can be sure that wherever you store something large—that will be the place you will need to work in.

You will always have to store some materials, otherwise you will not be able to work at all, but as a general rule never bring materials on to the site until you intend to use them. Not only will they be in the way, but they could get damaged or stolen. You will also be paying for them before you have to.

Site security

Something often neglected while doing this sort of work is security. You may enthusiastically smash out an old door or window and then discover at the end of the day that there is a large hole providing easy access into your house straight from the pavement. Anyone can then walk in and take your expensive tools and materials, and it happens all the time.

Therefore, you should try and plan to do all the jobs that will affect security of your property as early on in the course of the project as is possible. By doing this even if somebody breaks in there will be almost nothing worth taking. New doors and windows come into this category, and locks should be fitted as soon as possible. Don't forget to seal up any temporary means of access when you leave the site.

Work programme

A typical programme for a small site is shown on pages 70-71. The vertical column shows the various items of work and can include the contractor's name. The horizontal column shows the number of weeks that you expect the contract to run. Each box represents one week. All you have to do is to colour in the number of weeks you expect each item of work to take (based on the contractor's estimate), making sure that you space out certain sections of the work in order to avoid congestion on the site. It is obvious that preparation will come first and clearing the site will come last. It is also obvious that certain jobs can overlap—in fact they will have to, otherwise the job would never be finished in time.

Programme for a small site

Task \ Weeks	1	2	3	4	5	6	7	8	9	10	11	12	13	14	15	16	17	18	19
Scaffolding/preparation	▓																		
Structural brickwork		▓	▓																
Telephone			▓																
Fix steelwork/new windows				▓															
Damp-proof course				▓															
Remove old doors/plaster		▓																	
Roof work				▓	▓														
Electricity and gas						▓													
Internal partitions/alterations						▓	▓												
Wiring 1st fix							▓												
Lay solid floors/tiles						▓													
New manhole/drainage							▓												

Internal doors/woodwork

Strengthen and repair front steps

External render/repairs

Internal plastering

External plumbing

Skirtings and 2nd fix woodwork

Central heating and internal plumbing

Kitchen and bathroom fitments

Wiring/electrical 2nd fix

Painting internal/external

Garden/landscaping

Carpets/cleaning

Clear site

A typical estimate and schedule of renovation including labour and materials

Item	Cost £	Time
Scaffolding/preparation	1,200	1 week
Structural brickwork	900	1½ weeks
Site telephone (including calls)	300	—
Supporting beams (steel work)	350	3 days
New windows	1,450	3 days
Damp-proof course/timber treatment	1,400	4 days
Remove old plaster work/timber	180	2 days
New roof and guttering	1,900	2 weeks
New electricity and gas supplies	550	3 days
Internal partition work	900	2 weeks
Electrical installation	1,800	2 weeks
Basement solid floor and tiles	1,100	2 weeks
New manhole/drainage	650	1 week
Internal doors/woodwork	1,800	2 weeks
Strengthen/repair front steps and cellar	350	3 days
External sand/cement render and repairs	900	1 week
Internal plastering	2,200	2 weeks
Plumbing—internal/external	900	1½ weeks
Central heating/hot water	2,000	1½ weeks
Kitchen and bathroom fixtures	1,900	2 weeks
Painting/decoration—internal/external	1,900	2 weeks
Garden/landscaping	600	1½ weeks
Carpets	900	3 days
Skips/rubbish clearance	350	—
Cleaning/clearing site	200	2 days
Contingencies	1,200	—
Fees (solicitors/estate agents/etc)	2,500	—

The estimate and schedule lists the main items you are likely to encounter when carrying out a renovation. The amounts and the times quoted for each item will naturally be different when applied to different sizes and types of property and act only as a very rough guide here. However, this is the sort of list you should prepare (in more detail if you like) when doing your initial planning and costing. It is from this list that you make up your works programme. It is also the sort of detail that your bank manager and/ or backers will want to see, so you should try to be as accurate as possible without trimming it too finely.

Buying materials and hiring equipment

Having materials delivered v. collecting them yourself
If you shop around the wide range of builders' merchants and timber yards, you will find that the prices and quality of the goods for sale vary quite dramatically. So does the service. You can spend three or four hours running round trying to find a particular item from several shops giving poor service, queuing for 30 to 45 minutes in each shop, while in that space of time another will have taken your order by phone and delivered the goods to the site. Deliveries can be a time saver. Instead of wasting a whole morning getting tired and irritated you will have been able to use that time by working on the site or doing something else productive.

Free deliveries
Free deliveries are the rule rather than the exception, so there is a double incentive to use them.

Same day deliveries
For every type of supplies you need there is usually at least one merchant, particularly in the bigger towns and cities, who is much more efficient, helpful, and sometimes even cheaper than the others. You may well find that one of your suppliers can provide all of your materials and fittings for the entire job, ranging from sand and cement through to wooden mouldings and door furniture. Some places will take two or three days to deliver goods, and many will be reluctant to specify which day the delivery will arrive (problematic), but if you look around you will find the ones who will deliver the same day as the goods are ordered from them.

This has two positive advantages:

1. Same day deliveries avoid the risk of you (or your supplier) forgetting about making the necessary arrangements on the delivery date (ie, you to be there, him to load your supplies on to the truck on the right day)—it happens!

If you are involved with a lot of the work on the site, you will find that on some days there will be so many things happening at once that it is quite hard to remember everything (the surveyor and the health officers are guaranteed to turn up just when the phone starts to ring, and at the time you will probably be standing on one leg, holding up a half-hundredweight concrete lintel and trying to carry out measurements accurate to one-eighth of an inch). If something crops up which forces you to leave the site it's much easier to forget about an impending delivery arranged two days ago than one arranged only hours before. This may seem a small detail, but it's all the little things like this which can collectively become a major headache if not organised to minimise unnecessary frustration.

2. In our experience, the companies who are prepared to deliver on the same day as the order is placed with them tend to be more friendly and cooperative, as well as more efficient. They have usually gone out of their way to make themselves that efficient, and are very often smaller firms who are on the up and up because of their go-ahead attitude.

Many of the older-established bigger firms in the building trade, though not all, are hidebound by outdated working procedures and bored, unenthusiastic employees. In contrast to these dinosaurs are the new do-it-yourself supermarkets where most of the goods are on display and easily found by the customer; however, you must weigh against this the fact that they do not usually deliver goods and tend to be better for finished items, but rather pricey and inadequate for general items (see lists in appendix).

Hiring tools and equipment
Almost any of the tools and equipment needed on the building site can be hired. Apart from the most basic toolkit, eg electric drill, screwdrivers, hammers, bolsters, saws, tape measures, trowels, it is cheaper to hire than buy—you may only need some of them for a week at a time. You also save on the large quantity of storage space needed for stowage if you owned them all. Breakdowns can be less of a problem too—a replacement, at no extra cost, can be provided if equipment breaks down through no fault of your own, whereas having your own gear repaired or replaced causes either long delays or undue expense. Tools and equipment can also be delivered to the site.

Running the site office

You will need a site office of some description. Try to choose a room where the least work will take place, and equip it with a desk or table with a drawer and facilities for tea-making. If possible, you should also get a telephone. Ordering materials and hiring plant is made much easier if it can be done readily and quickly. It also enables others to contact you without delay—this may sound rather obvious but regular contact is important when running a business.

When asking for an installation, remember that a business telephone can be obtained more quickly than a private one.

In your drawer in the site office you should keep receipts, accounts, drawings and any other paperwork relating to the daily running of the site. All non-essential paperwork is better kept elsewhere to avoid clutter.

An important part of the daily running of the site is keeping accounts and records. You need to record all expenditure, including payments for materials, payments for work done by others and, of course, payments to yourself. It is worth making a record of transactions as they occur, even though you may be covered in mud at the time. Your accountant will want to see these records at some point, and they are particularly important if you have formed a limited company.

The more efficiently you run your site, the more smoothly the job will run, and others will respect your efficiency.

An office off the site

If you are fortunate enough to have the use of an office away from the site, maybe a spare room at home, you can equip it to a higher standard.

For a start, a typewriter is a major asset. Official letters always look better when typewritten, especially if you are using headed paper. A lot of confusion can be avoided by typing orders for materials, especially if your handwriting is a scrawl. A double order of kitchen equipment won't help your bank balance at all.

Always make sure that you have a spare cheque book in your office. There are few things more embarrassing than taking delivery of long-awaited supplies only to find that you have just used your last cheque for something else. Your materials will not be off-loaded, contractors and work will be held up, and you will have to arrange a temporary cheque book from your bank.

File all bank statements, planning approvals and letters. Make photocopies (or carbon copies) of any letters that you send, and file these. File contractors' invoices, tax deduction cards and books, and in fact everything relating to the business which you don't need to keep on site. Card files are adequate, but if you can get a proper filing cabinet—all the better.

Deal promptly with letters, especially to local authority departments, gas and electricity boards etc, otherwise they will lose interest in you and your project will be delayed. The Inland Revenue are also quite keen on prompt replies.

All financial transactions should be made from a bank account opened for business use only. This ensures that your personal money does not become involved and makes record-keeping much simpler.

It is unlikely that your office away from the site will need to be permanently manned. You won't need a full-time secretary, and incoming phone calls will be few and far between. However, there will be occasions when people need to get in touch with you. For this purpose it might be worth installing a telephone answering machine. It is only worth having one of these in your permanent office: on a building site it would soon be damaged.

Don't be tempted to spend too much time in your office, surveying your empire, as office work, although essential, is non-productive.

Keeping track of the finances

There will be some items which you will have to obtain yourself; it doesn't make sense to get a special delivery for the odd paintbrush or a bag of nails which you need *right now*, apart from the fact that even *asking* your friendly neighbourhood merchant is likely to go down like a lead balloon.

Cash kitty

You will have to keep a small cash float for these small items. £50 should be enough, although if you find that you regularly need more, don't practise the false economy of drawing so little out of your account at a time that you waste valuable hours standing in a long queue at the bank every other day to draw more.

However, a large quantity of loose cash on a building site can be a problem. Keep it in a separate wallet in your pocket as often as this is convenient, however much you trust your work-force; properties undergoing repair are invariably easy to get into during the working day, and there are moments when there is no one around to keep an eye on valuables left near an open door.

Cheque book
Your cheque book will do most of the work for you in keeping your cash flow records tidy and organised. You can open accounts with your suppliers if you wish, but beware the temptation to ignore how quickly the monthly bill is mounting up just because you don't have to think about it when making each purchase—you could be in for a nasty surprise at the end of the month and if you or your supplier have got your sums wrong, nobody will be able to remember exactly what happened on the day in question. Paying for every purchase separately, on the other hand, enables you to check the goods while the transaction is still fresh in your mind, and you can fill in a separate cheque stub for each as an added precaution.

If you get to know your regular suppliers they will let you pay for the goods with quite large cheques (£500 or more) without any hassles over your creditworthiness. This can speed things up considerably.

Accounting procedures

We have already discussed the importance when obtaining your start-up funds, of impressing bank managers etc with costings and projections. It is also vital to keep certain records of the ongoing finances of the project. This side of things can become unnecessarily complicated if you listen to the armchair entrepreneurs who are all too ready to advise you about money matters, whether you want the advice or not.

Here are a few suggestions for keeping the simplest possible records:

Day-to-day accounting and keeping a record of cash flow
The simplest and sanest way to handle the accounting procedures of the company from day to day, whether you are running the operation as a sole trader or through a limited company, is to keep three kinds of record:

1. *Cheque book stubs.* These should be filled in and preferably carry running totals of your bank balance on each; calculate it as each cheque is written, and you will have a means of cross-checking with your regular bank statements. If you *really* stick to a procedure of writing the amount of each cheque on the stub as you go along you will have a clear, easily evaluated record of your outgoings, for in addition to cheques for materials and labour, cheques

77

written for petty cash will also be shown. This also applies to the paying-in book; not many payments will be made into the account (apart from monies from people buying your properties) but there will be the odd refund on goods returned etc. Remember it's these odd transactions which slip through the system, so be warned!

2. *All receipts for purchases.* All receipts for goods and services paid for should be kept in date order. Quite a simple arrangement will do—a metal spike on a stand as used in offices will ensure that most of the time the date order is kept except for the odd, forgotten rogue receipt.

3. *A cash book.* This must show, as a minimum, cheques cashed for use in the cash kitty, which you will find is indispensable—there is always a host of small items which cannot practically be paid for with a cheque, ranging from half a dozen nails to a replacement for a broken tea mug. Your cash book entry for each cash purchase will give a cross-check with their receipts.

Management of cash flow
The job must be kept on the move by the availability of ready cash throughout its duration. From the word go, when you ensure before starting work that the money you have gained access to will be enough to cover the works, interest, a contingency figure (to pay for unanticipated work, at least 10 per cent of the basic costing), solicitors, surveyors and estate agents, you must know at any time whether or not you can afford to pay out more money on outstanding work to be done. Your budget must be adhered to.

Credit control must be practised. It is very difficult to reckon accurately how much you owe contractors if they are working on 'extras' which you have asked them to carry out, ie work which they have not estimated for but which turned out to be necessary when they finished the work which they *did* estimate for. Pressure of time often prevents an estimate being submitted—you will probably be very busy, and if the contractor has to stop working to draw up a costing he may not actually have time to do the additional work at once. He will probably have work arranged on other sites and may not be able to return to do the work for some time. Thus you may have arranged for these 'extras' to be done on a daily rate, ie you pay him an agreed sum for each extra day's work. If two or three contractors are undertaking this kind of work on your site, and you have been absentmindedly agreeing with their suggestions about work which they think necessary because you are so busy yourself, it's easy to run up an astronomical bill. So keep a weekly tally of these 'hidden' outgoings—they may not have to be paid until the work is completed but complacency will cost you dearly.

Additional accounting requirements for limited companies

If you are running your business as a limited company the requirements are more stringent than for the sole trader. As we have said, these are more than offset by the protections which limited liability provides.

You will be required to send the yearly returns to Companies House, showing the number of shares and shareholders in the company. You and your colleagues will probably be directors, as well as owners of the share capital, so these documents will show your current status within the company. The annual submission of these returns enables a check to be carried out on any changes in ownership of shares etc, and will be a mere formality in the early stages of the company's existence.

You will be required to produce annual company profit and loss accounts on a balance sheet which must be submitted to the Inland Revenue for scrutiny—your accountant will deal with all this, but remember that he will compile these documents from your own records (cheque book stubs, receipts and cash book), and you will have to pay him, so make his job as easy as possible.

Outgoings and income—some good points

One of the best features of buying and selling property and renovating it is that the book-keeping is simplified by the fact that income is not from a large number of sales of small items as in many self-employed businesses, but from a few sales of large items—flats and houses. Thus there is no problem with collecting unpaid debts, which can be a time-consuming and frustrating aspect of many business ventures.

Also, as you are managing the money yourself, how much of a wage you pay yourself, and when, are things which you can decide for yourself to some extent. However, the more you hold back on paying yourself the less bank interest you'll have to pay, and clearly if you exceed your allocation of wages in the early stages you will find it difficult to get back in step with it later. Again—be warned.

The most important aspects of finance and accounting

Consistent costing, estimating and budgeting before and during the operation are vital to the success of every project. However much flair for design you may have and however good a work force, if the finances get out of hand they can reach a point where profitability is no longer possible.

Chapter 10
The Work Itself—Some Practical Suggestions

So much for the organisation and management of your projects, but what of the actual nitty-gritty—the physical transformation of the property? Whether you are getting involved in any of the building work yourself or not, it is more than likely that you will be wondering what the most important dos and don'ts of a typical renovation/conversion are.

Although we do not intend to give a blow by blow account of all the practical aspects of the work, here are some general points: first you have to submit formal notice to the District Surveyor that you are about to start work. This is done on a standard form obtainable from his office.

Major items

There are several large items in an old, run-down property which will almost certainly need a major overhaul or complete replacement.

1. The roof

The roof will probably be suffering from several longterm leaks and the resultant damage and, in a house of 100 to 150 years old, it is worth considering re-roofing rather than patching up. A new roof, although not necessarily even seen by the prospective buyer of the property, is a good selling point. For instance, a new slate roof not only looks impressive on the surveyor's report (easily visible from the upper storeys of the house if on a single-storey rear extension, for instance), but the effectiveness of a patched slate roof is always extremely hard to judge (due to the means by which slates are fixed on the roof battens). The surveyor's eye can see at a glance if a new roof is weather-proof, hence he is much more likely to give it a clean bill of health. One of the problems with patching up is that the disturbances caused by the repairs can start new leaks in unreplaced sections; adjacent slates can get cracked when walked on, and flashings and soakers which have become porous over the years are prone to splitting.

We recommend that of any work which you decide to contract out, the roof should be given the most care. A good, reliable roofer will save a lot of aggro later in the job; leaks from a badly repaired roof have an unhappy knack of showing some time after completion of the work—tell-tale symptoms such as bubbling paint and crumbling plaster can be relied on to appear overnight just when you are about to show a prospective buyer around.

It will be useful to get the building weather-proof and give time for rain-damaged timbers and walls to dry out in the early stages of the project before some of the more delicate operations such as plastering, second fixings and decorating have to be carried out. Your roofer can be at work while you are getting the rest of the job moving. In fact he, along with the damp-coursing contractor, can be set to work as soon as the tracks have been cleared for starting the whole job (ie cash, and if necessary, planning permission and grants). If he is worth his salt he will be able to advise you on any structural work needed on the roof or if re-slating or re-tiling is sufficient. Leaks may have damaged the timbers, or old age might have caused them to sag.

A good way to check out your roofer if you have a slate roof is to observe his reaction to the suggestion that you should re-roof with tiles. This is a perfectly feasible thing to do, but tiles are much heavier than slates, and in almost all cases the roof would need to be strengthened to take the extra weight. If his answer takes this into account and he doesn't simply jump at the chance of making a quick buck by tiling on the existing timbers, it's a reasonable bet that he won't be the kind to take short cuts.

Don't be afraid to have a look at what he's doing up there from time to time; even if you don't understand it all, it shows you're concerned enough about the workmanship to keep tabs on even the most inaccessible parts of the property.

2. The damp coursing

This is the second most likely candidate for an outside contractor. The best companies give a guarantee, often of 25 years, for the work, and will deal with timber treatment for rot and woodworm at the same time. The quality of the service varies greatly between different companies. We recommend the companies mentioned in the appendix.

It is very handy to get the damp coursing done while the roofer is at work for the reasons mentioned in 1.

3. Solid floors

Any concrete or ceramic tiled flooring at ground level will have to be proven to be damp-proof to the satisfaction of the District Surveyor. In most cases, in this kind of property it will have been badly laid, or it will be uneven, worn and broken. You may well find the easiest thing to do is to pull the lot up, lay a concrete slab of 4 to 6 inches deep (consult the DS) on appropriate damp-proofing—pvc sheeting, or tanking of asphalt or similar material, and finish it all with a 2 inch screed of concrete. It usually costs as much to half do the job as to do the lot; if you need to mix more than 2 cubic metres of concrete, use ready-mixed—it is cheaper than mixing on site, much cleaner and less space-consuming (no lorry-loads of sand in the road for days, no bags of cement to 'go off' before usable), and much faster, sometimes a little too fast for comfort, in fact. You can get the delivery driver to pour it down a chute if, for example, you are flooring a basement, or if the site is not adjacent to the road, a pump can be provided by the firm supplying the concrete. Screeding can be done by hand-mixing or ready-mix, and should be done after the slab is dry enough to walk on and after any gas, water and electricity services have been laid on the surface of the main slab.

4. Heating

Gas central heating is by far the cheapest and most effective system available at present. It is a big selling point and refurbishing a house provides an excellent opportunity to install it. We strongly recommend it in areas where it is available. However, a detailed examination of the different types of heating systems and fuels is given on page 125, so a choice based on availability, cost and efficiency can be made.

5. Electricity and water supplies

Again, half doing the job is usually as time-consuming as installing a completely new system; a partly rewired electrical system will only be as good as its weakest components, and that odd section of antique wiring you decide to keep because it's inaccessible and seems to be working all right will be the first to cause problems in the new system. As with other items, complete replacement gives you the opportunity to rationalise its layout and bring it all up to a uniform standard, which is just not possible if you try to patch up a system which has 'evolved' in a piecemeal fashion over decades of changing technology and building practice.

The same applies to the water supplies and plumbing, including water storage tanks.

6. Floors—the joists

Don't spend a lot of time and money ripping out floor joists whole-sale just because a couple are rotten. Even if the floor is tilting it can be left as it is—most people are prepared to accept this as part of the charm of a period building. As long as the DS agrees that it presents or indicates no structural hazard to the building, any feature which would, in a new building, be criticised for being 'out of true' may well look more in keeping if it is slightly repaired at a jaunty angle rather than removed and rebuilt completely. The fur-ther you take the latter operation the more you run the risk of upsetting a sort of 'harmonious imbalance' that emanates from an old house in which walls have settled a little and doorways have moved.

It has been suggested by another writer that all the floors in a period property which is being converted should be pulled out and re-positioned to give equal headroom on each storey; instead of the original layout where, as the building is ascended, the ceilings become lower, the new floor positions would give ceilings of equal height on each floor, hence giving every unit adequate headroom. This is nonsense. The expense would be pointless. Apart from the inevitable loss of cornice mouldings on the lower floor(s), impres-sive ceiling heights of around 13 feet would vanish to make way for an average height of about 7 to 8 feet, with nothing accomplished; it is very rare, even in the top storey 'servants' quarters', to find impossibly low ceilings; often, low ceilings can be just as much of a selling point as tall, elegant rooms with ornate plasterwork. To the right buyer they can be more attractive, and dealt with imagina-tively give a cheap opportunity to remodel the geometry of the top storey into interesting shapes. This is discussed in 7, but one final point against adjusting floor heights: the original windows will be at the wrong level. It might even not be possible to see out of the top floor windows at all unless you stood on a chair!

7. Ceilings

If the ceilings on the top floor of the main part of the house or of the extension are in bad shape, don't just replace them in the same lay-out as before. You have now a good opportunity to 'open up' the ceiling.

Often the rafters upon which the old ceiling was supported can be cut away, and a new ceiling fixed to the sloping rafters which support the external covering of the roof itself, the slates or tiles. The shapes which this can produce look very pleasing. They also effectively increase your room sizes (check that the proportions 'work' though—you may find that the resulting rooms will look too tall for their width) which makes the whole dwelling look more spacious than before.

The possibilities don't end there: you can install roof lights, which are small windows set in the roof itself. Apart from making an interesting feature in the room they can be opened to give more ventilation as well as more light. A good point with roof lights is that they are now available cheaply—the smallest ones for as little as £30 each—from a variety of manufacturers. Most of them come with flashings and soakers and all the paraphernalia which used to make fitting them such a headache already attached. They are an outstanding bargain. Two good roof light manufacturers are included in Appendix 2.

Your ceiling can be finished in plasterboard and plaster or the attractive and inexpensive alternative of tongued and grooved boarding, which is easy to fit and can be clear varnished or oiled to give the 'Scandinavian' look.

All these refinements need cost little more than a replacement for the wet, sagging ceiling which had to come out anyway. One word of warning—don't forget to put your wiring and insulation between the rafters first! The air space in the original loft will have provided a measure of insulation against heat loss. That cushion is effectively removed by opening up the ceilings, so you must compensate for it by increasing the new insulation accordingly.

Other important features

Here are some points on how to deal with other key aspects of the property:

● Wooden floors

Some of the wooden floors in your house will be in very rough shape. It is notoriously difficult to find replacement floorboards which match the existing ones size for size—often each house of this age seems to have its own particular size of boards, while modern timber measuring systems use several different conventions, none of which comforts to the old sizes. There is also the difficulty of assessing sizes because of uneven wear.

The best solution to save you tearing your hair out by the handful and wasting time is to compromise with what you've got; settle for fully boarded floors (which can be sanded down and varnished) in some rooms, carpets, floor tiles or lino in others. This can be achieved by stealing boards from some rooms to provide ready-weathered, matching replacements for the missing and damaged boards in others. Kitchens and bathrooms, for instance, are excellent candidates for tiled or lino-covered floors. Pull up the old boards in these rooms and lay chipboard as a base for these finishes. This medium has a positive advantage over narrow floorboards in that it evens out differences in joist heights and gives a smoother surface on which to fit the tiles, as it has much fewer joints. Another plus is that inspection panels for plumbing checks and maintenance can be cut to exactly the required shapes and tiled over, with corresponding cut-outs in the tiling. This arrangement is virtually impossible with tiling on to floorboards, even if they are covered with hardboard first.

The age of the wood in the old floorboards gives them a rosy hue which is brought out by sanding and even more by each coat of varnish. Use a two-part varnish or sealant if you wish. We find that the better one-part polyurethanes (especially PU 15) are quite up to the job and less unpleasant to use.

● **The shell of the building**
This item is likely to be too costly to tackle in the earlier projects, but if your costings for the work permit, and if the outward appearance of the building is particularly grim due to years of accumulated soot and dirt coupled with the ravages of an acidic atmosphere, it may be worth getting in a contractor to clean the stone or brickwork. The transformation is staggering; anyone who has seen the difference in the appearance of buildings such as the Albert Hall after cleaning will appreciate the truth in this argument. An amorphous browny-black blight on the landscape becomes transformed into a glowing work of art. The same is definitely true, in more modest terms, of many period houses which have been cleaned up.

The main things to remember about having the outside of the building cleaned are first, that it is expensive—at the time of writing a typical three-storey house 40 feet high by 34 feet deep by 24 feet wide will probably cost over £3000—and second, that the windows will have to be covered during the work to prevent the glass dissolving—one of the cleaning agents used is hydrofluoric acid, which has the distinction of being the *only* acid capable of doing this.

Where brickwork is discoloured with age and pollutants but not painted, sandblasting is an alternative method of cleaning. It may cost as little as half the price of chemical cleaning, but can be even messier, as the sand used gets blown about by the wind and collects in heaps. Also, some local authorities don't approve. Your local Yellow Pages will have details of firms who carry out this kind of work, usually under 'stonecleaners and restorers'.

● Architectural features

If your property has some interesting architectural features don't dispense with them: draw attention to them by restoration. Most of these decorative elements, usually but by no means only external, adorning various doors and windows etc, evolved over a long period of time and are carefully proportioned to please the eye. They are often crafted in sand and cement mortar (or 'plaster' to use the general term for outside and inside finishes of this kind). It can, however, be expensive to employ someone with the skills necessary to refurbish these features and, in addition, there is often more repairing to be done than meets the eye, for once disturbed they often crumble away to nothing and must be replaced completely.

Fortunately, there is now available a wide range of replacements for these mouldings which are fabricated in fibreglass so authentically that it is virtually impossible to tell the difference between the genuine article and the imitation. Unlike most of the original mouldings, they are not made up in situ, but factory-made and simply fitted in position with screws.

There are several advantages to this type of moulding:

First, they are light and easily fitted in position, whereas fitting those in plaster not built in situ was and is a major operation due to their great weight.

Second, this reduces the number of people getting in each other's way on the site while fitting takes place.

Third, the quality of the workmanship is seen before the feature is installed—it can be soul-destroying, when your new plasterer has just rebuilt an important feature for you, to find that the result is not a great improvement on the original crumbling wreck. This may not be due to a lack of skill on the part of the plasterer, either; sometimes working conditions on the site can be difficult—if there has been a lot of rain (not an unfamiliar phenomenon in the British

Isles), there may be several people who have been delayed by it bustling around making up for lost time, but getting in his way, or the rain itself may ruin a masterpiece before the plaster has enough time to cure.

There is also a wide range of pre-formed mouldings available for interior use. Being made from expanded polystyrene these are also light and easy to fit in position with the adhesives supplied by the manufacturers, several of whom are mentioned in the appendix.

It is always possible to re-run cornices or rebuild ceiling roses, either in plaster or substitutes, but you can easily end up spending a lot of money (invariably more than you thought) on these items. On your early projects try cleaning up the existing ones with water and a small brush. You may find that layers of distemper are hiding some pretty ornamentation. We discovered that a row of amorphous blobs on a cornice was in fact, after cleaning, an extremely delicate array of tudor roses moulded in plaster of Paris. A member of the local historic buildings department explained that careful brushing with water would enable them to be prised away from the cornice, brushed clean and refixed with cove cement, which is quick-setting and prevents you having to stand all day holding one moulding in place until it is secure.

● **Skirtings, door frames and architraves**
Mouldings in wood present a similar problem to the renovator as to how much should be left and how much replaced. Many of the more elaborate skirting or wainscoting mouldings are irreplaceable if you are using ready-made off-the-peg styles, and having them made up by your local neighbourhood joiner is enough to induce palpitations of the cheque book. If you can't afford to do this, use the same arrangement as with the floors: collect together all the most exotic existing ones in the house and salvage the best-preserved sections; you can then use them to adorn the biggest, most ornately decorated rooms while fitting the more modest rooms with off-the-peg skirtings, of which there are some quite pleasant shapes available. One thing is for certain: nothing looks worse in a property which purports to have been 'renovated' than different styles of skirting board joined together on the same run of wall. Do it properly and the results will speak for themselves.

There is a slightly different but equally economical solution to revitalising tired door frames and the internal ornamentation on window frames. Most internal door frames consist simply of the 'lining', the 'door stop' and the 'architrave' moulding. Many renovators remove the lot and replace it all, but apart from the expense of all the new wood needed for this operation on all doors in the house, this is often unnecessary. It usually results in damage to the surrounding plaster, if not to the brickwork itself, which in turn can lead to a further 'infinite regress' of one job leading to another (an occupational hazard for the renovator). So nip it in the bud: the lining, which is simply a flat three-part frame (top and two sides), and which is there to hang the door itself on and to stop the walls from 'fraying', as it were, is invariably in sound condition except in the tattiest of properties. It is usually the architrave which gets the most battering. This is the almost invariably fluted moulding which overlaps the join between the lining and the edges of the plaster on the wall. If this is replaced with a new one, the transformation of the whole frame assembly is miraculous. The stop will probably need replacing as well—it will probably have been joined badly in several places—for it also gets fairly heavy wear and tear and it costs nothing to replace. The 'new architrave' method also works very well on window frames which look beyond the pale, particularly those which are set in panelling. The architrave is only nailed in position and can be carefully prised away from the frame assembly to make way for the new one.

Your local neighbourhood joiner will make up any specialised skirtings which you feel you cannot do without despite the expense.

● Windows

When you are trying to save the pennies, windows present one of the biggest problems of all in renovating a period property. There is no satisfactory short cut when faced with a senile sliding sash window assembly—it's tempting to try and refurbish damaged glazing bars and fill gaps in the woodwork rather than replace the whole assembly, but when you work out just how much time you spend overall to get a very average result (on an old sash window it is virtually impossible to sand down paint-clogged woodwork to a smooth finish without horrendous expense) it's cheaper to have a new one made up. This despite costing over £200 on a 4ft by 3ft assembly including costs of fitting sash cords and weights; the sizes are all different; almost every window in one of these houses is likely to have different dimensions from the others, and there may be several different glazing patterns (the layout of panes in the frames). Spending this much money may hurt but it pays off in the appearance and saves a lot of frustration and elbow grease at the painting stage, for the surfaces are satin smooth. A useful tip is to get your joiner (there is one near you—just look in the Yellow

Pages) to paint them with primer before delivering. It may well be raining in the period after installation for some time before you can get around to doing it yourself, and once the woodwork is wet the sashes will jam due to swelling.

We much prefer, even when installing additional windows to a house, to use period-style windows in keeping with the age of the premises. This used to mean custom-building by the joiner, but some of the mass-producers of joinery, eg Magnet and Southerns, are expanding their ranges to include ready-made assemblies of this type, mainly Georgian so far. Their uses are limited as they are restricted to several specific sizes, which is, of course, how they can be so competitively priced. They may be useful where a new rear extension is being added to the property, for the available sizes can be 'designed into' the new work.

Suppliers of mass-produced joinery can be a cheap source of plain sashes, ie simple frames which are set into the walls and glazed. They can be cut to different sizes easily. We have found them useful for forming inspection windows through which a row of gas and electricity meters installed behind them may be read; thus the meters can be read from outside the building without having to be fitted in bulky and ugly boxes on the outsides of the walls.

There is one position in the house where ready-made windows of a different style from those originally fitted may be used without a glaring visual clash, and that is in newly dug-out basements; these are seldom visible from the kind of distance where one tends to see the building as a whole. There are some excellent double-glazed units available with aluminium frames coated in unplasticised pvc with a white finish which makes painting unnecessary. Double glazing is more of a priority in a basement than in the rest of the house, which tends to be warmer anyway, and in this position advantage can again be taken of the opportunity to use off-the-peg sizes to cut costs. Companies of special note are mentioned at the back of the book.

● Plastering

Many renovators replaster throughout from scratch. This is unnecessary. As long as plaster has not 'blown', ie become detached from the walls—probably due to damp, it is possible to put a smooth finishing coat of new plaster on top. Consult a good plasterer on this one—sometimes plaster, although still adhering well, may be crumbling due to sheer old age.

● Fireplaces, fires and woodburning stoves

If your budget permits, it is well worth looking into the possibility of installing at least one period fireplace in each unit of accommodation. You may be lucky enough to have found a property to renovate or convert which has its original fireplaces intact or needing just a minimum of restoration. Stove black paint on the cast iron and a little quick-setting cement such as Prompt Cement or Jetcem around broken marble and stonework will often suffice to bring a tatty, neglected specimen back to life. Don't waste time trying to repair a broken casting—it will never look as good as the original or a replacement, and it won't stand up to the heat of a fire. The same applies to broken fire-bricks which are difficult to match size for size with new ones.

Even if you are fitting central heating, it is worth considering going the whole hog and making the fireplace as much of a focal point in the room as it used to be, as a source of heat and the relaxing sight of flickering flames. Today's log effect gas fires look much more like a real log fire than their predecessors of the last 30 years or so; in fact, it's almost impossible to tell them from the genuine article. The heat output is only modest, however, and they are expensive to run, but what a perfect showpiece to help sell your property!

An alternative which has a double advantage over this system is to install a woodburning stove. First, rather than needing an ornate fire surround to set it off, which is the best setting for the log effect fires mentioned above, the woodburning stove is in many cases an ornate piece of furniture in its own right. You can use this to advantage—the fireplace need be no more than a rectangular opening at the base of the chimney breast, large enough to house the stove, or you can even stand it in front of the chimney breast. This works particularly well in combined kitchen-dining rooms where the slightly primitive appearance of the stove enhances the workmanlike feel of the surroundings. Fuel is easily available for these stoves even in the heart of the city so there is no problem with running them—building sites are a copious source of well-seasoned timber, and sawmills and woodyards produce a continual flow of unwanted offcuts which the proprietors will be pleased to see the back of. In fact, as a renovator you would have ready access to vast quantities of reject timber from your sites, so you might well want to install one in your own home.

The second advantage of the woodburning stove is the heat which it puts out—much more than an open fire. Some of the

Norwegian Jotul stoves put out 9 to 16 kilowatts, which is as much as five double bar electric fires. Ash rarely has to be raked out as combustion is so efficient with the stove doors closed that the fuel is nearly all turned into heat. As a result no smoke is produced, so that these stoves may be used in smokeless zones.

If you are considering tackling a country cottage renovation or conversion these stoves are particularly practical. In many country areas there is no mains gas. This makes cheap central heating impossible—electricity is expensive, and bottled gas is too. A woodburning stove is easily installed in an existing chimney—it makes a beautiful feature of an old inglenook fireplace while cutting the heat losses of an open fire by 60 to 90 per cent; the wood stove puts out about five times as much usable heat as the open fire. In the country it is possible to run the stoves on wood obtained by coppicing of the hedgerows, fallen trees, and possibly unwanted ash trees owned by the Forestry Commission, which have already been allowed to fall to make way for new planting.

The value to the renovator of these remarkable stoves lies in the following: the doors on most models may be left open to provide the sight of a real fire; smoke need not be a problem if dry, well-seasoned wood is burned (one advantage of using old timber from building sites); many models will burn hot for up to five hours or so on one filling, and stay alight overnight; some models have facilities for heating hot water systems and several radiators; and finally, there is no need to chop down all the trees in the street to keep warm. Without even having recourse to the supplies of ready-cut firewood (you can never be sure if forests are being decimated with no replanting schemes) available in most areas, the above-mentioned sources can supply all the user's needs. Hence these stoves can be quite a selling point if their location is carefully thought out beforehand. Look out for these models and you will see how they can be both decorative and functional:
—The Kosi Gee and Ophelia by Lange (Danish)
—Some of the Jotuls (Norwegian)
—The Marlborough by Logfires (English).
More details are given in the appendix.

A rough guide to comparative costs:
—Small cast-iron period fireplaces start at around £120.
—Wooden fireplace surrounds, ie mantel and side pieces, start at about £130.
—Log-effect gas fires can be bought for as little as £150.
—Woodburning stoves of reasonable quality start at about £260.

If you have gas supplies available but prefer the look of a wood-burning stove, as from 1988 these stoves are also available fitted with gas burners and thermostats. This development permits either individual room heating and temperature control from a series of separate stoves, or with the larger units a central heating system run from one large woodburning stove, in the living room, for instance.

● The new electrical installation

Instead of wire fuses, fit miniature circuit breakers to the new consumer unit (what some people call the 'fuse box'). Unlike the wire in a fuse, they do not need replacement after blowing when a fault occurs. They switch the current off in the event of a fault, and can be subsequently reset after the problem has been solved simply by switching them on again just like an ordinary light switch. This takes literally one second, compared with 10 minutes or so to replace the wire in a fuse, not to mention the time spent hunting for the right fuse wire and going to buy some if you have none left. MCBs are an immense help both to the builder and the future owner of the dwelling.

Electric night storage heaters which use cheap nighttime electricity have recently been redesigned. They are now slimmer and less obtrusive, and although once they are hot the heat output cannot be completely shut off (they heat up at night and give off the heat into the atmosphere during the following day) controls enable the rate at which heat is dispersed to be adjusted, which has virtually the same result. This system is well worth considering, unlike its predecessor, where the heaters had no controls at all and often sent temperatures soaring into the high 90s if a warm day followed a cold night when the householder had switched the heating on in anticipation of a cold spell.

If using this system, provision should be made at the wiring stage for a separately wired circuit with appropriately positioned outlets in each room and the separate metered supply which night storage heating requires. Your local electricity board will have more details.

● Improving security

Many people feel the need to make their homes more secure these days, and replacing doors and windows which have reached the end of their useful life enables the installation of new period-style units which can be obtained ready-fitted with anti-burglar locks.

Many such items are available as complete door-and-frame assemblies with latches and locks, saving hours of installation time and several fruitless journeys in the search for compatible fittings.

Where replacement of such features is unnecessary, or undesirable owing to the lack of a suitable substitute (no self-respecting renovator would discard a two-inch thick original carved oak front door which could be patched to replace it with an inferior copy pre-fitted with a cluster of Chubbs and Banhams) it's well worth bringing the premises up to a uniformly high level of protection against intruders. Although the owners of more grandiose dwellings may require alarms, bells, warning lights, room scanners and a hot line to the local police station, safety precautions needn't be expensive on early or small projects. Sash window lock assemblies as required by most insurance companies only cost £2 or £3 per window and are easily fitted during the building work. Such details may help to tip the scales with a prospective purchaser who might otherwise hesitate with pen poised over the contract of sale.

Homes in less secure areas may well need more obvious security devices than mere locks and alarms. Window grilles and steel or iron gates, particularly where garden or basement flats are positioned close to alleyways and the like, not only provide a more visible deterrent but also make the owner feel more secure. People living in an area like this feel more able to hold a conversation with their neighbour and leave the front door open because a gate in front of the open door can be locked, allowing light and fresh air in with no risk of the family silver disappearing.

A little forethought in fitting such devices during the refurbishment of the property can make them less conspicuous than when added as an afterthought. This applies particularly to items such as window gates. In preference to unsightly fixed bars cemented into the external walls, these gates run on tracks and are located on the inside of the window. They can be drawn back like the gates in older-style lifts, or like shutters, to leave the window uncluttered when there is someone at home or when they are not required. They are made up specifically to fit each particular window—a security firm in your area will be able to supply them. They are normally fitted ready-painted, which helps them to blend in with the surrounding architecture.

Landscaping and irrigation
When restoring a property with a garden, the temptation is often to consider it of secondary importance to the property itself. It is

often used for dumping rubbish and storing materials, and will probably look like a piece of waste ground once the property renovation is complete. This is a pity because the garden *is* part of the property as a whole, and does play an important role when it comes to selling. In fact, a properly landscaped garden can, on its own, be the deciding factor for someone buying the property.

Landscaping need not be elaborate. A simple scheme could include a small paved area—or patio—flower beds and a lawn. A grander scheme might include such items as trellis-work—maybe to hide a blank wall—a rockery, raised flower beds, a pond, a brick-built barbecue (gas-fired if you like), and a few shrubs and climbing plants (although filling up the flower beds too much probably isn't a good idea). A prepared garden ready to receive the lavish attention of the horticulturally minded house buyer not keen on doing the donkey work would be a major selling point.

You can go further still.

It is possible, and certainly not difficult, to irrigate a garden to any extent required by burying water pipes under the ground which feed spraying devices concealed in flower beds and lawns.

For a lawn, pop-up sprinklers are used. These simple devices rely on water pressure to force the spray nozzle out of the ground and water the grass. When the water is turned off they retract to just below ground level and are almost invisible. For flower beds permanent above-ground sprays can be used.

The whole system can be connected to the main water supply (or a tank), and a pump if necessary, and can be controlled by a time switch to water the garden automatically as often as required.

Obviously, burying pipes under the soil is not as easy in an already laid-out and flowering garden. Combining it with the general renovation work is worth considering, having assessed the merits of such a system in relation to the property being renovated, the size of the garden, cost-effectiveness and so on.

Summary

This chapter does not pretend to be exhaustive in its discussion of practicalities. You will have plenty of ideas of your own about what to do and what not to do, but the points mentioned here may help to set you thinking about the things which must be considered, both large and small.

Chapter 11 discusses the most important of these issues in relation to completing your first project.

Chapter 11
The Finished Product

Your first project will probably be a conversion into flats. When the work is finished you should have a saleable commodity on your hands.

What makes the property saleable? Try to see it through the eyes of a prospective buyer. Young couples buying the first home of their own will be impressed by a flat which looks fresh, cheerful, spacious and comfortable. A plethora of expensive kitchen gadgets and fittings, immaculately restored period fireplaces, exotic ceiling roses and the like do look impressive, but they all cost a lot to install and are best not indulged in too much on the early projects. A very pleasing effect can be created simply by tastefully finishing off aspects of the work which are essential anyway— there is nothing to beat well-finished basic plasterwork and joinery for giving an elegant appearance to even the most modest of dwellings.

The first impression

Don't forget that, although most of your work will have gone into putting the building itself to rights, the appearance of the property in its surroundings as approached from the street will create an important first impression. Tidy up the garden. If your pocket will run to it, 'landscape' it with a few shrubs and, if possible, a couple of jardinières on the window sills. Repair any damage to garden walls and fences, and give the garden gate a lick of paint. Make good the path leading up to the front entrance, and the front steps. All these things help to enhance the setting of your property. They have a strong impact on the buyer, for they create a more comfortable environment for the home.

The front door gives you an excellent opportunity to show your taste before your clients have even entered the house. Brass door furniture—the doorknob, knocker and letterbox—will give it an elegant appearance and set the tone for what the viewer will see inside.

Builder's finish

In our opinion at this stage of the game it is safest to decorate the entire interior of the property in white, for several reasons:

● It shows off good new plaster-work to its best advantage, reflecting more light than any other colour, and making the whole place look fresh and cheerful.

● White makes rooms look spacious, bigger than they really are— a highly desirable quality.

● White is generally acknowledged to be the standard 'builders' finish', and is less controversial than others. It is notoriously difficult to appeal to other people's tastes with colour schemes of one's own choosing, and it will be a needless waste of time and resources to have to redecorate from scratch if your own brilliant combination of colours should put off would-be buyers. White is neutral and tends to be a 'non-colour', so play safe and use it.

Decorate walls in a recently replastered building with white emulsion; this acknowledges, and will be seen to acknowledge by those who know, ie surveyors acting on behalf of potential buyers, the fact that new plaster takes several months to dry out—there is a saying in the trade that for every inch of thickness of a brick wall you should add another month for drying out, (ie nine months for a 9 inch thick wall, and so on). Emulsion will allow this moisture to dry through the paint to some extent, whereas paper will eventually peel and leave you with a distinctly unimpressive finish to explain away to your clients. Thus, using white emulsion implies that you are aware of this and merely providing what may only turn out to be a temporary but presentable decor.

Original features

We ourselves like to preserve *some* original features of the building, even when finances are hard pressed. The notes in the previous chapter dealt with most aspects of this subject, but it is worth mentioning that if you can salvage nothing else already in the house when you first acquired it, two items may be worth keeping and drawing some attention to in the finished product:

Panelled doors
Wooden panelled doors look much more attractive than the oft-fitted flush (flat) ones made from hardboard and cardboard. They

feel better, they have the right weight, and although in some cases you may have to put fireproofing in the panels (not difficult) you will find that you will be able to reuse many of the doors already in the house. The odd missing one can be replaced with a second-hand door from your local neighbourhood pine-stripping shop where there will always be spare ones available at a nominal price. Round them off with brass knobs, which will beautifully complement the white paintwork.

The original floorboards
Bearing in mind the points made in the previous chapter about floors and having made up complete wooden floors in some rooms, you will find that there are quite large gaps between the old boards due to loss of natural moisture and shrinkage over the years. These gaps can be filled with a mastic filler, easily and quickly applied with a hand gun. The filler remains flexible after it has cured, or 'gone off', allowing for further shrinkage of the boards. It comes in different colours, so you can use a brown mastic if you want it not to show, or white if you want to emphasise the joints.

NB. A general footnote on woodwork and central heating
Remember that central heating gives a very dry heat which will cause such loss of moisture content in wooden fittings of every kind that they will soon warp and, in the case of panelled assemblies literally tear themselves apart (this includes the doors and floors, of course). So do your buyer the courtesy of pointing out that humidifiers are needed to counteract this effect, even if you don't actually provide them yourself.

Importance of the kitchen and bathroom
Apart from the general appearance of the interior the most important rooms to 'get right' in a conversion or renovation are the kitchen and bathroom. We have mentioned that lavish appointments are out on the first projects, but a little style with the essentials will achieve a good result. Both rooms must be provided with storage facilities—kitchen worktops and cupboard units, airing cupboards etc, and it is now possible to buy stylishly finished units in kit form from very cheap sources; for example, the MFI range has been much improved of late and yet the prices are still pegged very low, with realistic wood-grained finishes and good colour options available on elegant designs.

In addition to the atmosphere that these units can help to create, your choice of bathroom suite, kitchen sink design, wall and floor finishes (probably tiles) can sell the place almost on their own in many cases. Style combined with restraint and economy is the keynote.

Cork floor tiles. Cork tiles pre-sealed with a veneer of clear pvc are an excellent way to finish the floors of rooms which are likely to have a lot of water splashed about in them, and may easily be laid over rough wooden floors by glueing them to a backing of hardboard which has been nailed to the floor first. While these tiles are not cheap, the speed at which they can be laid compensates for this, and their universal appeal ensures that you won't be putting anyone off by using them. Be sure to buy the tiles which are already coated in pvc—the others are useless. They have no strength and, even after varnishing in situ, soon become soggy and break up.

Bathroom suites and how to save money on them. A white bathroom suite is considerably cheaper than this year's 'in' colours. Most dealers also do a range of 'budget' colours which cost a little more than white but a lot less than the Kashmir Beiges, Indian Ivories and the like. These budget colours—usually yellows, greens and pinks—can look quite presentable in the right setting, although obviously not as plushy as the luxury colours. Even the clinical look of a white suite can be softened in carefully chosen surroundings.

Carpets. Many estate agents will insist that the only way to sell a property easily is to fit carpets throughout. This is fine, but they are expensive, and the estate agents don't have to foot the bill. Estate agents are keen to make their commission by quick sales, and not necessarily so keen to maximise your profits.

In some cases, fitted carpets may put off would-be buyers who are keen to strip the floors themselves to give the property more of a 'natural' feel. On the other hand, if you decide to patch up the existing boards and leave them ready to be stripped if the buyer wishes, *or* to be carpeted, hence wasting no expenditure on unnecessary preparation, this is often seen by viewers of the property as skimping on the work and again they may be put off if your choice of colours is not to their own taste. Also, old floorboards which may be quite good enough for stripping and varnishing don't look particularly impressive before this has been done, so if you leave them in this condition you also run a risk of putting some people off, even though you may simply be keeping their options open.

It is surprising how little imagination the average homebuyers have in this and other areas of decor—they instantly know what they don't like when they see it, but are less sure about how they would have done it themselves. If you are unfortunate enough to have the more demanding kind of viewer looking at your property, it is worth remembering that invariably the most awkward ones are those who are least likely ever to get around to buying at all. It is really not worth spending hours with this kind of client and offering to make all kinds of alterations to get a sale. They are notoriously unreliable, and the next time they see you they will probably have changed their mind anyway. Fortunately, one learns how to spot them a mile off at an early stage of the game and behave accordingly.

The decision as to what to do with the floor treatment in the property is one of the trickiest of the project. It's really for you to weigh up the cheaper alternatives against what really suits the 'feel' of the property best; we *have* sold flats with floors hard-boarded ready to receive carpets, but it's a hit-and-miss business. The safest colours for fitted carpets are beiges.

Lighting. It's tempting to let your imagination run riot on the lighting, with carriage lamps outside the front door, brass wall lamps in the living room, and panoramic strip lighting under the worktops in the kitchen. But your tastes may be different from those of your buyer, and it is not a pleasant business, in a complete conversion or renovation with neatly finished floors, to have to pull them up and re-run cables. This is what you will be faced with if your fabulously expensive wall lighting arrangements leave him or her cold and a centre ceiling light is preferred.

Unfortunately, any attempt at pre-wiring to cater for any of several different lighting positions still doesn't solve the problem—in our experience things still seem to be 'in the wrong place'. It is better to eat humble pie and stick with straightforward centre lamp positions as far as possible until you progress to catering for the penthouse set!

Consumer law

Consumer law has only a minimal effect on property sales. Once he has the surveyor's report the buyer is deemed to be in possession of all the relevant facts regarding the property, and the purchase is then made 'as seen and approved'.

However, if you have installed guaranteed items such as a damp-proof course, central heating, kitchen appliances etc, it may be necessary, as a condition of sale, to agree to repair or replace defective parts during the guarantee period, especially if you have installed these items yourself. So make sure you keep all receipts relating to guaranteed items in a separate file.

If you employed contractors to install, for example, central heating, the buyer of your property may have to arrange through you the implementation of any work under guarantee, as you were the one who initially paid for the installation.

Guarantees for damp-proofing and dry rot protection ought to be transferable to the owner of the property. The reason for this is that such guarantees are usually lengthy (20 years or more) and the property could be sold and resold several times during the guarantee period. So you should make sure when employing damp-proofing contractors that their guarantees *are* transferable.

You should offer guarantees to your buyer on anything which you bought or installed that carries a manufacturer's guarantee. This may involve you in a little time but should cost you nothing more than the occasional phone call or letter.

Chapter 12

Marketing and Selling

Fixing the selling price

If you researched your project thoroughly at the start, you will have known all along what sort of price to expect for the finished product.

However, what you planned on paper doesn't always compare with what happens in practice. You may find that the quality of your renovation surpasses the standards you set yourself initially, which will, of course, increase the value of your property. On the other hand, the finished product may be less than you hoped for. The uncertainty of the exact final value put upon the conversion is one very good reason for not over-estimating the selling price when you do your initial costing.

It is the actual finished product that your buyer looks at, and with a critical eye.

The best way to get a market value put on your property is to get one or more local estate agents to look at it, whether you intend to use them to sell the property or not.

Being used to selling properties in your area, they can give you an immediate idea of market value, nearly always based on what, for example, a 'two-bedroom flat in the area' is worth, with added points for garden, carpets, fitments, quality of finish etc.

Having decided on this market value, it is then necessary to fix an advertising price. This should always be over and above the market value because anybody interested in buying is more than likely to make an offer which is nearly always below the asking price. This little charade ensures that you get somewhere near to the market value for your property, and the buyer is happy because he has achieved a 'discount'.

If you are lucky enough to have several people making offers at the same time, you are in a strong position and can hold out for the highest bid.

It is highly likely that the person who wishes to buy your property will have to obtain a mortgage. This will take time to arrange, so if you have somebody interested in buying who has cash available (maybe from a recent house sale), it is well worth giving them special consideration, even if their offer is slightly lower. The faster you sell the better it is for you.

Methods of selling

As mentioned earlier, in the case of conversion into flats it is sometimes possible to finish one flat in advance of the others and sell it, even though the rest of the flats are far from finished. A prospective buyer may exchange contracts subject to completion, which will normally entitle you to a 10 per cent deposit. An inflow of cash at this stage of the renovation is not to be sneezed at, and if buyers are that anxious for your flats it proves that you have chosen your area and layout well.

Once your property is finished you will want to sell it as quickly as possible. A property sitting on the market for any length of time will cost you money in the form of bank interest and deterioration. So before the work is completely finished you must decide how to sell — or market — your property.

There are various choices open to you, and these are:

● **Selling to friends**
This is a satisfactory way to sell as you avoid advertising and estate agents' fees.

● **Advertising yourself**
National newspapers, local papers and property magazines are relatively cheap forms of advertising and it is well worth trying this form of advertising before any other. The big Sunday papers bring in the best response.

● **Computer selling**
For a fixed fee (based on the selling price) they will circulate details of your property to people interested in that type of dwelling, for as long as necessary.

● **Property shops**
You put a card in their window with property details. Good value for money, but reaches fewer people.

● **'For sale' board**
As well as advertising elsewhere, you can erect your own 'for sale'

103

board outside the property. You can put on it as much detail as you like about the accommodation, and you can also include the price — something that estate agents' boards don't often do.

It's worth mentioning here that, due to public outcry about the environmental mess caused by the proliferation of estate agents' boards, new legislation is due to come into force at the end of 1988 to reduce the size of the boards from the present 2 square metres down to 0.5 square metres (approx 700 mm x 700 mm).

Current legislation already restricts the number of boards to one per unit, and in some areas boards are not allowed at all. Any local authority wishing to implement this legislation can apply to the Department of the Environment for permission.

● Auctions

These are not the best places to sell renovated property. Auctions are better for selling cheap unmortgageable properties.

● Estate agents

Last but not least. Definitely the best way to tap the largest possible market in the shortest possible time is to put your property with several estate agents (not just one). They are obviously very experienced in selling property quickly.

The drawback with using estate agents is, of course, the large fee that they require to sell your property. You can pay as much as 3 per cent of the selling price. This means that on the sale of three flats at £60,000 each you would pay £5400 in agents' fees, and that is a large slice out of your profits, so if you can sell by other means — do so.

Freeholds/Leaseholds

When putting your property up for sale, you will have to decide whether or not to sell the freehold.

If you wish to keep the freehold yourself it means selling your property on a lease; the length of the lease then has to be decided. It ought not to be less than 99 years. By keeping the freehold yourself the value of the property will be reduced, and you will be responsible for collecting ground rent and possibly liable for some of the general upkeep of the property. It is generally better, therefore, to include the freehold in the sale of the property.

In the case of a single property, renovation of a house for example, this is easily done.

In a flats conversion it is not quite so straightforward. Leases are normally granted on each flat and then someone has to own the freehold. This someone could be yourself, or one of the lease-holders, or all leaseholders could jointly own the freehold. Your solicitor will advise when drawing up the leases, and in consultation with the buyers and yourself.

In our opinion it is better for you that the freehold is sold with the property.

Chapter 13

Legal Requirements Relating to the Business

Company law

If you propose to conduct your business as a limited company, you will be required to register it with Companies House. You can decide on a name, and purchase the company for about £200. You can if you wish buy an existing company, but this is generally more expensive and complicated.

One of the most useful features of a limited company is that it gives you the protection of limited liability: if your business should go seriously awry, you will not then be held personally responsible for paying any outstanding debts still owing after all the company funds have been exhausted. This contrasts with, for example, running your business as a sole trader, or in a partnership, where your own personal finances could be seized by a debtor.

The price you have to pay for this protection is more red tape. You are legally required to issue a certain number of share certificates to yourself and partners (these will not actually be partners in the legal sense—they will probably be your fellow directors in the company. In legal terms, a partner is part of 'a partnership', which, as mentioned above, is less well protected than a limited company). You must also appoint directors, hold annual general meetings and send 'company returns' to Companies House every year. You will also need to appoint a company secretary—here you may be able to kill two birds with one stone by appointing your solicitor to this post if he is amenable. This will cut down the amount of liaison necessary between people, saving time and money.

The company will need a Memorandum and Articles of Association, which is merely a description of the trade(s) which the company is legally entitled to carry on. Your solicitor will prove his worth once again by dealing with this for you.

Apart from such general obligations pertaining to the limited company, the property renovator is compelled by the law to conform to other conditions and restraints.

The local authority

You will have to carry out any work done on your property in accordance with local authority requirements, including building regulations and the by-laws.

Compulsory repairs

These may be required if the Health Department has put an order on the premises condemning it as unfit for habitation. If the owner fails to carry out these repairs within the authority's specified deadline, it is free to have the work done and charge him for it—at a much higher figure than it would have cost him to organise it himself.

If it is considered dangerous as well, the authority may even slap a demolition order on the property.

If an order for repairs *has* been put on the house, don't automatically be put off buying it. Most of these you will be aware of and will be intending to carry out anyway. However, it pays to have a thorough investigation done in this area (which is taken in by your solicitor's local authority search—see Chapter 4), as the vendor and his solicitor may well not be falling over themselves to point out these shortcomings to you.

In some cases, however, these orders are somewhat over-zealously applied; a couple of years ago we were interested in purchasing a mews cottage which seemed to have a lot going for it until we discovered that, in addition to our planned works, we would be forced to carry out re-roofing and major underpinning, neither of which we considered necessary. A health order was in force. The project was, therefore, not financially viable, so we had to look elsewhere for our next purchase. A grant might have been available for these items but in view of the problems we describe in Chapter 2 with reference to grants, we gave it a miss.

Searches and conveyancing

At the beginning of the project, the local authority search is required by law. As things stand at present the search and conveyancing are carried out by the solicitor in most cases. You can do them yourself but they take some getting to grips with.

Contracts and solicitors

At present each party in a property transaction must have his own contract drawn up, which he then passes to the other party for signature. Also, each party must have his own solicitor. There may be new legislation on the way enabling just one document and one solicitor to perform the transaction, thereby saving both vendor and buyer money, time and frustration. The legal profession will still manage to scrape a living, even so, and it will leave a little more money in the renovator's pocket for the work in hand.

Listed buildings

Another control you may have to contend with is the listing of buildings which are considered to be of architectural and/or historic interest. The grade 1 or 2 listing of a building means that anyone repairing or modifying it may be obliged to spend money on restoring some of its historic architectural features to the specification given by the relevant DOE department. This work may well have to be financed out of the renovator's own pocket, as listed building repairs grants are becoming increasingly hard to obtain (see Chapter 2 on raising finance).

The sort of features involved in this kind of architecture are certain kinds of mouldings and decoration, eg pilasters, porticoes, colonnades and corbels; typical glazing patterns characteristic of definite periods of architecture, eg Regency, Georgian, Victorian, Edwardian (often, over the years, repairs will have been carried out which mix incompatible styles, and the historic buildings officials will press to have the original period features restored); and details like front door styles and garden railings.

Most of these regulations are applied much more rigidly to the outside of the building rather than the inside, certainly on the properties which come within the newly established renovator's funds. When your fortunes have grown enough for you to start renovating Scottish castles, it will be a different matter!

Highways regulations

A more mundane legal restraint on you, but none the less one to be reckoned with once you start the renovation proper, is exerted by the highways regulations.

During the course of the work you will be receiving deliveries of heavy, bulky materials—bricks, sand, cement, slates, lintels etc—which cannot be moved or stored easily. A vast quantity of rubble and rubbish will have to be removed from the site by skips or trucks. You must observe the by-laws by obtaining a permit for any materials or skips to be left in the road. The only strings attached are that they carry a time limit. Once a permit has lapsed it must be renewed if still needed.

The highways officers are surprisingly quick to notice even a few odd bricks left on the pavement for a couple of days, so get yourself covered before they show up. Delays due to this kind of interruption can be irritating and disruptive to the progress of the job.

In some circumstances a permit is also needed for scaffolding erected over a pavement.

Insurance

Public liability insurance
Any building site is, by the nature of the work, prone to accidents from time to time. You must have an insurance against any injury sustained by a member of the public in an accident on or near your site. Anything might happen—a passer-by might be hit by a falling scaffold board—and a large claim would severely detract from the project, let alone make a dent in funds if the worst came to the worst.

The law requires any subcontractor who wishes to obtain a Tax Exemption Certificate (see Chapter 8) to take out such an insurance. The minimum cover is about £250,000. As main contractor, you should take out your own, even though your 'subbies' may have them. The premium would be around £70 a year.

Insuring yourself and your tools
While you are at it, insure yourself for loss of earnings due to injury, and your tools against theft; at least *one* of these items is irreplaceable.

Insuring the property
If you have a bank loan, the bank will require you to take out an insurance against damage to the property during your ownership. They will be happy to organise one for you. In any event, you *should* organise cover for the premises or you might find the carpet well and truly pulled from under you financially if anything should befall it.

Chapter 14
Venturing into France

The phenomenal rise in the value of property in Britain has been an important factor in influencing many people, particularly those looking for second or retirement homes, to consider buying abroad. The popularity of Spain for Britons seeking retirement and holiday homes is well established, and other countries, France and Italy included, also have a lot to offer in this respect.

France's proximity allows frequent and relatively inexpensive visits. Its other main attraction is the variety of its landscape, from the generally flat but picturesque north, through the greatly differing central regions, the mountains and the coastal areas in the south and south-west.

If you are interested in taking the plunge and buying and renovating in France then, as in Britain, the amount of initial research that you do is important and will reveal a lot of basic essential information. Speak to foreign property agents based in Britain (listed in Appendix 2), who have lists of available properties and can arrange viewing trips. It is also worth contacting a solicitor used to handling foreign properties. A list of such solicitors can be obtained from the Law Society in London.

The standard of living in France is high. Property prices, however, are generally lower — perhaps due in part to the fact that the country is much larger than Britain, and yet has a smaller population. Whatever the reasons, the fact is that there are plenty of properties available. The would-be renovator is hard to please if, somewhere along the line from farm cottage to château, he didn't find something suitable to renovate.

It is important to stress that the following pages give only a detailed outline of the subject of buying in France, the procedure to adopt, and some of the problems that may be encountered. They are intended to give guidance to those wishing to find out more.

Where to start

If you are tempted to buy and renovate in France, then a good way

110

to begin is with a small country cottage in either Normandy or Brittany. There are plenty of these available and prices start at about £8000 (March 1988) for one in need of complete renovation. Take, for example, a two-storey stone cottage. The following is typical of what would be needed to restore it:

- New roof and supporting timbers
- New floors—ground and first
- Making good the stonework and repointing
- New windows
- Partitioning for bathrooms, bedrooms etc
- Electrical wiring
- Kitchen
- Bathroom
- Heating (central heating or room heaters)
- Drainage (septic tank etc)
- Decoration
- Garden/landscaping

If a fireplace and chimney exist they should be repaired and usable, as in rural areas there will be plenty of wood available for burning. Also, in rural areas, a mains gas supply would be unlikely, so kitchens would have to be equipped for electric or bottled gas appliances. Central heating tends to be electric for the same reason.

Area

When choosing an area in which to buy, bear in mind that you will have to sell or let it when it's finished unless you want to keep it for yourself. If you intend to sell it as a second, or holiday, home, then your prospective purchasers will want to be able to make good use of the facilities of the country they are buying in. They will want to use their cottage for long weekends and short breaks. As such, a place not too far from a small town, a beach or an area of historic interest would be more enticing than one miles from anywhere.

It will be more sensible to gear your renovation for sale to the English rather than the French. In practical terms the finished product won't be that much different, whoever you sell to. The 'local style' should be maintained, for example, although internally a different 'look' may be needed for the English eye, with regard to kitchen layout, wall and floor tiling, and bathroom equipment. It is difficult to go into details, as style and 'feel' are personal things, but it would be a good idea to have a look at a few modernised properties, just to see what can be done.

The reasons for aiming your renovation at the English rather than the French are that:

- There is a well established market
- There will be fewer language problems
- You can advertise in Britain, either personally or through French property agents based in Britain (listed in Appendix 2).

However, if a French buyer comes along first, then sell to him! You will, of course, need a local (French) agent who holds a key, and who will show the property to prospective buyers, whatever their nationality.

If you intend to let your property you should still gear the renovation to the English market, because the prices that you will want to charge will not attract French people. You will need a local managing agent, who will, needless to say, take commission for handling your property. Letting would mean that you would retain ownership of the property, and it would therefore be available for your own use, but check on commission rates and letting potential before committing yourself.

The buying procedure

So—how do you go about buying in France? The legal procedure is more straightforward than in Britain and the method is as follows:

(a) You have selected your property and wish to proceed with the purchase.

(b) You make an offer to the vendor. If the offer is accepted then the agent or a *notaire* is contacted in order to draw up a preliminary contract, known as a *compromis de vente*. A *notaire* is employed by the state to carry out conveyancing for both vendor and purchaser, and does approximately the same as solicitors in Britain. In this country buyer and seller each have their own solicitor, whereas in France the *notaire* acts for both parties.

All land and property in France is registered with the *cadastre*, which is the equivalent of the Land Registry in Britain. The *cadastre* operates in conjunction with the *Conservation des Hypothèques*, which keeps a register of mortgages and any charges which may affect the property that you intend buying.

(c) The next step is to pay your deposit (normally 10 per cent) either to the *notaire* or to the estate agent. The deposit is paid under conditions drawn up in the *compromis de vente*. This has to be signed, preferably in the *notaire*'s or agent's office. Once this agreement has been signed a contract exists between buyer and seller and, unlike the British system, gazumping cannot take place. On the other hand, of course, both parties are now committed to the sale—so before signing the agreement make sure that all your finance is available.

As a foreign buyer all your finance has to come from outside France. You normally open a foreigner's bank account in France and pay for your property in French francs converted from sterling. The reason for this is that when you sell your property the monies paid to you can be brought back to this country under exchange control regulations.

Payment by either of the following methods is acceptable:

● Arrange with your British bank to transfer money directly to the *notaire*'s account.
● Organise a bank draft.

Whichever method you choose, ask your bank to advise on the details.

Between the signing of the agreement and the completion of the sale a period of time elapses (normally a few weeks) in which planning searches are made and 'title' is confirmed by the *Conservation des Hypothèques*. The French land commission (SAFER) has the right to buy any agricultural land over 2 hectares (about 5 acres) as soon as it comes on to the market, so a period of time must be allowed for them to decide whether they wish to purchase, and completion cannot take place until they have declared their intentions.

The planning office issues a *certificat d'urbanisme* which states whether any developments are intended (roads, buildings) which could affect your property. They will also tell you what sort of developments are allowable.

Although signing the preliminary agreement commits both purchaser and vendor to the completion of the sale, the purchaser usually has the right of withdrawal from the transaction (and has his deposit refunded), provided the clauses are in the agreement, if:

- The SAFER pre-empts, which means they intend to acquire the land
- The *certificat d'urbanisme* shows that your property could be affected by intended developments and/or planning acts.

A draft copy of the sale document (*acte de vente*) must be presented to the purchaser by the *notaire*, and must be checked by the purchaser. Ask the *notaire* to explain anything that you don't understand or that is incomplete (if your French is good enough).

If you have been wise enough to have engaged a solicitor in Britain who is used to dealing with foreign properties, then get him to check documents and transactions at every stage of the deal, and obviously before signing anything. A few hundred pounds spent in this way will avoid mistakes and misunderstandings and also help quell any fears which may arise from having to cope with legal documents in a foreign language. It is strongly recommended.

(d) Completion. If you have spent time and money on cross-channel trips already, you can avoid another one by getting the *notaire* to appoint someone to sign the completion document on your behalf.

The final signing takes place in the office of the *notaire*.

The purchaser pays over the remainder of the agreed price (the purchase price less the 10 per cent deposit) to the *notaire*. Fees must also be paid at this stage (see *Fees and charges* below). All the fees are paid by the purchaser. The vendor has nothing to pay. Unfair as this may seem, the position is of course reversed when you resell the property and become the vendor.

Once the monies have been paid and everything is in order, the final document, the *acte de vente*, is signed. The purchaser is then the legal owner of the property and takes possession, and the vendor receives the amount due to him. The signed document has to be sent away to the Land Registry. The *notaire* handles this formality and presents the duly registered document to the new owner when it is returned.

Fees and charges

As a rough guide, the cost of conveyancing, stamp duty and land registry fees amount to about 10 per cent of the purchase price on properties over five years old—less for newer properties.

The charges are made up as follows:

- *Notaire's* fees   approximately 3 per cent
- Land Registry fees ⎫
- Stamp duty (including ⎬ approximately 7 per cent
  various other taxes) ⎭
- VAT is included in the
  charges

Estate agent's fees. These are fixed by law in France, and a scale of fees can be inspected at their offices. For the type of property we are concerned with here the fees would be about 5 per cent. These fees are normally paid by the purchaser, but in some regions of France the vendor pays, and in others it is shared.

Renovating the property

Even if your French is quite good you will have to familiarise yourself with some of the building and technical terms needed in order to buy materials and equipment, fill in forms and correspond with the authorities, etc.

You may be tempted to export materials from Britain, maybe from known suppliers. This may work well enough with larger items such as kitchen units and bathroom suites, but it is better to use local (French) suppliers for such things as windows, roof slates, bricks, stone, etc, as these will be available in the local style. Keeping to the local style is important in that you need your renovation to fit in with the surroundings, which in turn will attract buyers. Few people want to cross the channel to discover imported bay windows and polystyrene ceiling tiles. In addition, importing materials and equipment from Britain will require customs declaration and may incur additional VAT payments.

Building applications and permission are dealt with by the town hall (*mairie*).

If you intend to do all the work yourself there is no need to apply for a *carte de séjour*, which is a resident's permit, but if you are setting up in business and intend to employ others, a permit will be required. If you do intend to employ people, either locally or from Britain, then you should consult your accountant regarding your tax position. It is advisable to do this anyway, before starting any property purchase transactions.

Selling your property

As with the selling of all property, the faster it can be done the better it is for all concerned. Selling abroad may not be as easy as it is in one's own country, especially if you are not able to be there all the time. Ideally, your property should be on the market while you are still in the country so that you yourself can advertise it and be there to show around the interested parties.

If at all possible, plan the completion of the renovation work and therefore the marketing of the property at the most favourable time of year (March to October). Apart from the fact that weather conditions are better, many potential buyers will be on holiday in France anyway, and will have the time and the inclination to look at available properties. If you cannot be in the country all the time, you will have to leave a key with a local agent.

You can advertise your property through French estate agents, British agents specialising in French properties, and British newspapers and magazines. Avoiding the estate agents will, of course, avoid their fees.

The higher the price you ask for the property, if it is to be a holiday home, the more difficult it will be to sell. By their nature, second homes have to be reasonably priced because the amount of time spent in them is very limited, so don't spend too much time or money on the renovation. As with properties in Britain you must tune the quality of the renovation to the market available.

When a buyer is found, the process of buying and selling is the same as when you purchased. It is advisable to use the same *notaire* that you used previously, as he will have a record of your first transaction. This time round, of course, in your role as vendor, you will have no legal charges to pay.

Taxes

Income tax. Obviously you must consult your accountant about your own tax position. Your status, whether operating your business from France or Britain, may be significant, although buying a second house in France is unlikely to involve you with French income tax. There is a double taxation agreement between France and Britain. Letting may involve French tax authorities.

Capital gains. Selling your property within two years of purchase will necessitate payment of capital gains tax, which is deducted from the proceeds of the sale by the *notaire*. Keeping the property for more than two years reduces the tax liability year by year.

VAT. France has a high rate of VAT (18.6 per cent) which is included in conveyancing charges. It is also charged on materials bought locally and persons and companies employed locally. There is also a higher rate of 33⅓ per cent on some luxury goods.

Local rates. These vary from place to place but are generally lower than in Britain.

Travel

Travel between Britain and France, as anyone who has done it will know, couldn't be easier. The car ferries ply from various points on Britain's south coast to the French ports known to most holiday-makers—Calais, Dieppe, Le Havre, St Malo, and so on.

Hovercraft cross more quickly, but only on certain routes.

Air travel is also available, for example in northern France, to Le Havre, Caen, Deauville and Dinard.

The Channel tunnel is due to be completed in the early 1990s. Apart from making the crossing simpler, it could be an incentive for British people to buy property in France.

Finance

You can borrow money in Britain on the security of your British residence or other assets, but not all British banks will lend for the purchase of foreign property. French banks can lend to foreign buyers. They will lend up to 50 per cent of the value of the property, and a popular method for foreign buyers is to finance 50 per cent of the sum required in France and 50 per cent in Britain. However, the rules relating to borrowing can change at any time, for better or worse. Interest rates and the franc/sterling exchange rate can also change, so when setting up finance make sure that all the influencing factors have been taken into account. Always consult your accountant before committing yourself to any deal.

Finally, if you decide to go ahead and buy the 'place in France' you will not be alone. A chat to one of the French property agents in Britain (page 136) will reveal just how many people do buy abroad. There are even English builders working in France, renovating for those English people who have bought property but don't have the time, the skills or the inclination to do it themselves.

Chapter 15
How to Use Profits and Plan Ahead

Of those that set themselves up in the property business by borrowing capital, all but the most adventurous will start by buying one property, doing what they want to it, and selling it before they contemplate anything further. This is certainly the safest and surest way and is to be recommended.

Having completed and sold your first property, however, and assuming that it has worked reasonably well, you will be keen to go on to the next one.

It is still advisable, and probably necessary financially, to stick to one property at a time. You would need to build up considerable capital and expertise to be able to handle several properties at once. The amount of expertise depends upon the individual, of course, and you could be faced with the option of expanding your business and borrowing more money, or staying with the smaller conversions and using your profits.

Assessing your first renovation

If you made a reasonable profit on your first renovation and you wish to go on to something bigger and better, bear in mind that you should still keep well within your financial limits. You will in any case have to consult with your bank and/or backers.

Your financial backers will naturally evaluate your success in terms of profit, quality of renovation, ease of selling etc, and assuming that you have managed your first project competently, will be bound to want to continue with their support. A successful businessman will always attract backers.

With your first property out of the way, the risk is that you become over-confident.

Sit down with your site diary, works programme, financial projections, estimates and costings, and evaluate for yourself how successful you were. Note down where mistakes were made; where estimates were wildly out; where, perhaps, something was not allowed for at all. The experience gained from this will help enormously with your next project.

This is also the time to reflect on the contractors that you used. How punctual were they? How competent? How many call-backs were necessary to put something right? Would you use them again?

You can also assess your own ability at doing certain jobs, and whether it would have been quicker and cheaper to employ specialists. It may have been that you wished to do the work yourself in order to gain practical knowledge. If you have achieved this it will benefit you next time whether you do the work yourself, or not.

By renovating one property at a time and assessing your results in this way after each one, you will become very experienced and discover that expanding your business will present little difficulty.

You may be tempted to try and work out a comprehensive plan for the next five to ten years. Forget it. You must treat each project as a separate entity, and allow events to take their course. 'The best laid plans . . .'

Using profits

When your first project is finished and sold, you will have a large amount of money in the bank. Some of it will be borrowed money, some profit. What you do with that money will depend to some extent on how you set up the finances in the first place. For example, if you have not been paying yourself a regular wage (just expenses), you may need to draw some money for yourself. Your backers or partners may need to do the same.

You are faced with the problem of how much, if any, money to withdraw, and how much to reinvest, or roll over, into your next property. Obviously, the more money you put into the next property the less you will have to borrow, and the greater the possibility of tackling something larger. The bank may agree to increase the amount they will lend. In a purely business sense, it is better to reinvest as much as possible in your next property, and it will look good on paper.

If you do intend to draw out some of the profit (as opposed to expenses) it is a good idea to have a chat with your accountant about the best way to do it, as you will attract taxation in various forms, and he will explain how to keep it to a minimum.

There is another way of using profits, although you may have to wait a year or two and acquire some capital to make it possible. Assuming that you already own the house you live in you can, in addition, buy a house or cottage (maybe in the country), modernise it to a reasonable standard, and then hang on to it until you retire (it might be sooner than you think).

The benefit of doing this is that when you do retire, you can sell either the house you have been living in, or the one you have been keeping as an investment. This provides you with a sizeable capital sum to supplement your fixed pension. The longer you have owned your investment property the more it will be worth.

You will be liable for capital gains tax on one of the properties but it is still worth doing.

Also, of course, by living in town and buying your investment property in the country, you have the choice of either place to live when you retire, and a weekend retreat in the meantime.

New technology

New products and materials are continually coming on to the market in the building industry, and you will obviously be tempted to use some of them. You will need to be careful about how far you go with new materials, as a lot of potential buyers of your properties will hold traditional views and will not be impressed if new products have not been tried and tested.

Plastics, for example, are increasingly being used in place of traditional materials for windows, roofing products, tile and brick-effect walls, central heating pipes, and so on.

Glass fibre, although not new, is increasingly being used instead of plaster and sand/cement when replacing or newly installing porticoes, cornices, columns, pilasters etc. It has the advantage of light weight, and speed and ease of installation. It also requires no maintenance.

The microchip is also making inroads into the home (particularly in electrical control equipment and security systems), and in the next five to ten years is bound to affect the design and renovation of buildings.

New technology and products always take time to become accepted into everyday use, and before using anything untried in your properties you will have to decide for yourself what is acceptable and what is not.

Keeping in touch

While attempting to buy your first property you will have encountered a few estate agents. Some will have been friendly and efficient, others maybe a bit offhand and unconcerned. It is in your interests to keep in regular contact with estate agents, preferably the friendly ones. Stopping off at their offices occasionally will keep you in touch with the market generally, and them in touch with progress on your property.

Agents may be able to suggest minor additions or improvements to your renovation, as they are continually meeting buyers, and know what is popular and fashionable. They will also know whether the type of property you are renovating is increasing in demand and value, even while you are working on it. If it is, it may enable you to upgrade the property further, with the prospect of increased profit.

During these chats the subject of further suitable properties for conversion will undoubtedly arise. Such properties frequently come on to the estate agents' books, and if you are in regular contact you will be among the first to hear about them. Even though you may not be in a position to buy your next property there and then, there is no harm in going to have a look at those that sound promising. 'Just looking' will help you keep your ear to the ground and your mind focused on what your future moves ought to be.

Appendices

Appendix 1
Cost Comparisons for Central Heating/ Hot Water Systems

Comparison charts of running costs for central heating/hot water systems in domestic properties are available from several sources for such fuels as gas, electricity, solid fuel (coal), LPG (liquid petroleum gas), oil, and even solar panels. They usually show a 'typical house' or 'typical flat' with 'average' occupancy.

There are, however, so many factors affecting running costs that it is almost impossible, and certainly unwise, to attempt to predict the running costs for a system in a particular dwelling.

So we will attempt here to list the factors which affect running costs, and some of the advantages and disadvantages of various fuels.

Running costs

Reductions in running costs can be made for systems, no matter which fuel is used, if certain basic requirements are complied with. The factors which will reduce running costs are:

- Insulation—loft and cavity wall
- Double glazing
- Draught-proofing
- Properly designed and installed systems
- Corrosion inhibitors
- Regular servicing
- Effective time and temperature controls
- Sensible room temperatures

Conversely, running costs will be higher if insulation and draught-proofing are poor, systems are badly installed and maintained, the controls are insufficient (resulting in fuel wastage), room temperatures are excessive and there is heavy daytime usage. (This applies particularly to electric heating.)

Some properties are more prone to high running costs. A detached house on an exposed hillside, for example, will need more insulation, and cost more to heat, than a similar terraced property in the centre of a town or city. However, the factor which is most difficult to establish or determine is how the system will actually be used, and what people regard as a comfortable level of space heating. Older people, for example, generally need more heat than young. Some properties are occupied intermittently and others continuously. Whatever the requirements of the occupiers, renovation of a property should incorporate features which will favourably influence running costs.

Installation costs

However difficult running costs are to determine, the opposite is true of installation costs. Detailed estimates can be obtained for different types of systems using any fuel (subject to area availability) for any property. Estimates should come from reliable sources. Bear in mind that when using oil or liquid gas, a storage tank and access for deliveries will be required—factors which may affect installation costs considerably.

Fuel comparisons

Gas
The most popular fuel for domestic central heating/hot water systems in Britain.

Advantages
- Economic usage
- Low maintenance
- Speed of response to systems controls
- Ease of use

Disadvantages
- Expensive initial installation
- Unavailability in some areas

Electricity
Electric central heating normally consists of storage heaters which take in off-peak (night-time) electricity, and gradually release it as heat during the following day. The storage heaters have a limit to their intake, and if all the heat is used up during the day then ordinary heaters using peak-rate (day-time) electricity

have to be used instead. The latest storage heaters, however, have separate convector and storage provision, which allows the same unit to be used for either off-peak or peak-rate electricity. Therefore, if electric heating is used to its maximum, then running costs will be significantly higher than for other fuels.

Advantages
- Low installation cost
- Minimum upheaval
- No water leak problems
- No boiler or flue
- No maintenance

Disadvantages
- Slow response to controls (heaters using off-peak electricity need a night-time charge before they will work)
- The high level of insulation necessary for practical usage
- Higher running costs

While on the subject of electricity it is worth mentioning electric boilers. These can be used where, for example, gas is not available and fuel storage is not possible. An electric boiler can be linked to an ordinary 'wet' system (radiators heated by hot water), in the same way as a gas boiler. Running costs are obviously higher, but it is a solution if other fuels are not possible. There is also the added benefit that no maintenance is necessary.

Oil
Oil prices rose significantly a few years ago as a result of political conditions in some oil-producing countries, and have remained uncompetitive since. An option where gas is unavailable. The installed system is the same as for gas or solid fuel, ie a 'wet' system—only the boiler is different.

There are no particular *advantages* in using an oil-fired boiler.

Disadvantages
- The storage tank necessary in the garden or adjoining land
- High running costs
- Fuel deliveries

Solid fuel
Suitable if there is sufficient storage space. The installed system

is the same as for gas or oil—a 'wet' system using radiators and water tanks—except for the boiler, which burns coal nuggets or briquettes. Running costs are comparable with gas.

Advantages
- Open fires/room heaters
- Heating and hot water from a back boiler (limited by size of property)
- Can be linked to gas or oil systems (giving choice of fuels)

Disadvantages
- Regular filling and cleaning-out of boiler, coupled with the necessary bucket-carrying—not for the elderly
- Fuel deliveries

Liquid petroleum gas (LPG)
Standard 'wet' systems run on ordinary gas boilers converted to burn liquid petroleum gas, can be the solution where natural gas is not available.

Advantages
- The same as for natural gas

Disadvantages
- The large storage tank necessary in the garden or adjoining land
- Fuel deliveries
- High running costs

Solar heating
Installation in a suitable property is not difficult. The prospect of generating your own hot water is exciting. Yet there are just not enough suitable properties. When you need the hot water most (in the winter to run your heating system), there is insufficient sunshine to supply your heating needs independently. You still need the back-up of a gas or oil-fired system. There can be some benefit from hot water in the summer months, but at this operational level it can take years to recover the installation cost.

Aga
No examination of heating/hot water systems would be complete without mentioning the legendary Aga. As well as being a cooker

the Aga can be used to heat water, and a matching boiler is available for central heating. They can be run on natural gas, LPG, oil, or solid fuel. They are generally suitable for the larger kitchen, and make an ideal focal point.

Not surprisingly, fuel suppliers' comparison charts for running costs do vary, so when reading them study the small print and the criteria used to determine their figures. Probably the best insurance against high running costs is proper insulation and effective system time and temperature controls.

Useful Addresses

National telephone dialling codes are given, though local codes may differ.

Local councils and Chambers of Commerce can be good sources of help and information.

General

Alliance of Small Firms and Self-Employed People
33 The Green, Calne, Wilts SN11 8DJ; 0249 817003
British Gas
Rivermill House, 152 Grosvenor Road, London SW1V 3JN;
01-821 1444
British Safety Council
62 Chancellors Road, London W6 9RS; 01-741 1231
British Standards Institution
2 Park Street, London W1Y 3WE; 01-629 9000
Building Centres
26 Store Street, London WC1E 7BS; general enquiries
0344 884 999
115 Portland Street, Manchester; 061-236 9802
Earl Street, Coventry; 0203 25555
18 Cumberland Place, Southampton; 0303 27350
Hope Street, Liverpool; 051-700 8566
and other major towns and cities
Central Electricity Generating Board
Sudbury House, 15 Newgate Street, London EC1A 7AU;
01-248 1202
Consumers Association
14 Buckingham Street, London WC2N 6DF; 01-839 1222
Electrical Contractors Association
34 Palace Court, London W2 4HY; 01-229 1266
Health and Safety Commission
Regina House, 259 Old Marylebone Road, London NW1 5RR;
01-723 1262

Health and Safety Executive
25 Chapel Street, London NW1 5DT; 01-262 3277
HM Customs and Excise
VAT Administration Directorate, King's Beam House,
Mark Lane, London EC3R 7HE; 01-626 1515; and local offices
Inland Revenue
Contact your local Inspector of Taxes to register for PAYE and
find out where your Local Employers' Unit is for all necessary
paperwork (PAYE and National Insurance).
The Law Society
113 Chancery Lane, London WC2A 1PL; 01-242 1222
Registrar of Companies
Companies House, Crown Way, Maindy, Cardiff CF4 3UZ;
0222 388588
102 George Street, Edinburgh EH2 3DJ; 031-225 5774
43-47 Chichester Street, Belfast BT1 4RJ; 0232 234121
Solid Fuel Advisory Service
Hobart House, Grosvenor Place, London SW1X 7AW;
01-235 2020

Firms providing damp proofing and timber treatment service

Dampcoursing Ltd
10 Dorset Road, London N15 5AJ; 01-802 2233
Peter Cox Group Ltd
Wandle Way, Mitcham, Surrey; 01-640 1151
Rentokil Ltd
43a Selsdon Road, Croydon, Surrey; 01-686 9291

Manufacturers of products in general use

Access Irrigation—garden watering and spraying equipment
Crick, Northampton NN6 7XS; 0788 823811
Aga—cooking and heating equipment
PO Box 30, Ketley, Telford TF1 3BR; 0952 641100
Airflow Developments—airvents for rooms and toilets
Lancaster Road, High Wycombe, Bucks HP12 3QP; 0494 25252
Alpine Co Ltd—double glazing
Alpine House, Honeypot Lane, London NW9 9RU; 01-204 3393;
dial 100 and ask for Freefone Alpine
Armitage Shanks Ltd—bathroom equipment
303 High Holborn, London WC1V 3JZ; 01-405 9663

Barlo Products Ltd—radiators
Barlo House, Foundry Lane, Horsham, West Sussex RH13 5TQ; 0403 62342
Black & Decker Ltd—power tools
Westpoint, The Grove, Slough, Berks SL1 1QQ; 0753 74277
Calor Gas Ltd
Head Office, Appleton Park, Riding Court Road, Datchet, Slough, Berks SL3 9JG; 0753 40000
Carradon Terrain Ltd—plastic soil, waste and rainwater systems
New Hythe Lane, Aylesford, Maidstone, Kent ME20 7PJ; 0622 77811
Celcon Ltd—thermal building blocks
Celcon House, 289 High Holborn, London WC1V 7HU; 01-242 9766
Crabtree Electrical Industries Ltd—electrical equipment
2 Jubilee Way, London SW19; 01-542 4272
Cuprinol Ltd—treatments and stains for wood
Adderwell, Frome, Somerset BA11 1NL; 0373 65151
Delmar nmc Ltd—decorative mouldings
Manor Royal, Crawley, West Sussex RH10 2XQ; 0293 546251
Dulux Trade Group, ICI Paints—paint and woodcare products
Wexham Road, Slough, Berks SL2 5DS; 0753 31151
Everest—double glazing
Everest House, Sopers Road, Potters Bar, Herts EN6 4SG; 0707 875700
Faral Tropical 80—high output radiators
Tropical House, Charlwoods Road, East Grinstead, West Sussex; 0342 315757
FEB Ltd—sealants, adhesives, mortar additives
Albany House, Swinton Hall Road, Swinton, Manchester M27 1DT; 061-794 7411
Franke (UK) Ltd—sinks
Suite 15B, International Office Centre, Styal Road, Manchester M22 5WB; 061-436 6280
Glow-worm TI Ltd—central heating boilers
Nottingham Road, Belper, Derbyshire DE5 1JT; 077382 4141
Gyproc Ltd—plasterboard and insulation
Whitehouse Industrial Estate, Runcorn, Cheshire WA7 3DP; 0928 712627
Henkel Home Improvement & Adhesive Products—mortar additives, sealants and adhesives
Stanhope Road, Yorktown Industrial Estate, Camberley, Surrey GU15 3DD; 0276 685345

Hodkin & Jones (Sheffield) Ltd—decorative mouldings
Dunston House, Dunston Road, Sheepbridge, Chesterfield,
Derbyshire S41 9QD; 0246 455255
Ideal Standard Ltd—bathroom equipment
PO Box 60, Kingston upon Hull HU5 4JE; 0482 46461
John Carr (Sheffield) Ltd
Wood House Mill, Sheffield S13 9WH; 0742 693291
Kango Wolf—power tools
PO Box 379, Hanger Lane, London W5 1DS; 01-937 3444
Maxton Boilers—electric boilers
Consort House, Jubilee Road, Burgess Hill, Sussex RH15 9TL;
04446 47626
MFI Furniture Centres—budget kitchens and furniture
Head Office, 333 The Hyde, London NW9 6TD; 01-200 8000
Mira (Walker Crossweller & Co Ltd)—showers
Whaddon Works, Cheltenham, Glos GL52 5EP; 0242 527953
MK Electric Ltd—electrical equipment
Shrubbery Road, London N9 0PA; 01-807 5151
Myson Domestic Products Ltd—radiators and heating equipment
Ongar, Essex CM5 9RE; 0277 362222
Myson Heating Ltd—central heating equipment
Eastern Avenue, Team Valley Trading Estate, Gateshead,
Tyne and Wear NE11 0PG; 091-487 1021
PC Henderson Ltd—garage doors and sliding doors
Ashton Road, Harald Hill, Romford, Essex RM3 8UL;
04023 45555
Permanite Ltd—roofing bitumens and solutions
Mead Lane, Hertford, Herts S613 7AU; 0992 550511
Pilkington Bros plc—glass manufacturers
Selwyn House, Cleveland Row, London SW1A 1DN;
01-930 5672
Potterton International Ltd—central heating equipment
Portobello Works, Emscote Road, Warwick CV34 5QU;
0926 493420
Rawlplug—wall and cavity fixings
Rawlplug House, 147 London Road, Kingston upon Thames,
Surrey KT6 2NR; 01-546 2191
Runtalrad (1970) Ltd—stylish, made-to-order radiators
Ridgeway Industrial Estate, Ridgeway Road, Iver, Bucks;
0753 655215
Sadolin (UK) Ltd—wood protection
Tower Close, St Peter's Industrial Park, Huntingdon, Cambs
PE18 7DR; 0480 50041

Sphinx Tiles—range of wall and floor tiles
Bath Road, Thatcham, Newbury, Berks RG13 4NQ; 0635 65475
Stelrad Group Ltd—central heating equipment
PO Box 103, National Avenue, Kingston upon Hull HU5 4JN;
0482 492251
Thermalite Ltd—thermal building blocks
Thermalite House, Station Road, Coleshill, Birmingham
B46 1HP; 0675 62081
Twyfords Bathrooms—bathroom equipment
Lawton Road, Alsager, Stoke on Trent, Staffs ST7 2DF;
0782 29531
Ubbink—roof lights (windows)
Available from Preedy & Sons, glass manufacturers
4a Ashland Place, London W1M 3JH; 01-935 3988
Velux Co Ltd—roof lights (windows)
Gunnelswood Road, Stevenage, Herts; 0438 312570
Verine Products Co Ltd—decorative mouldings
Folly Faunts House, Goldhanger, Maldon, Essex CM9 8AP;
0621 88611
Volex Electrical Products Ltd—electrical equipment and
accessories
Accessories Division, Leigh Road, Hindley Green, Wigan,
Lancs WN2 4XY; 0942 57100

Large builders' merchants

C P Hart & Sons, Builders' and Plumbers' Merchants
Arch 213 Newham Terrace, Hercules Road, London SE1 7LD;
01-928 3812
Magnet & Southerns, Windows, joinery, doors and accessories
Head office: Magnet plc, Royd Ings Avenue, Keighley,
W. Yorks BD21 4BY; 0535 661133
Head office: Southerns Evans Ltd—Widnes, Ditton Road,
Cheshire WA8 0PP; 051-424 5500; over 240 branches
nationwide
Sandell Perkins plc, Builders', Plumbers' and Timber Merchants
Cobtree House, Forstal Road, Maidstone, Kent ME20 7AG;
0622 70111; branches throughout London and the south of
England
J H Sankey & Son Ltd, Builders', Plumbers' and Heating
Merchants
London office: Unit 1, Humber Road, London NW2;
01-450 3377; many branches

UBM Goslett, Builders' Merchants
  Warwick Place, High Street, Uxbridge, Middx UB8 1HL;
  0895 38200; and branches
M Wisepart Ltd, Builders', Heating, Plumbers' Merchants and
  Kitchens
  Factory Lane, London N17 9BY; 01-801 2161; and branches

Tool and equipment hire shops

HSS hire service shops
  over 70 branches and depots in England, Wales and Scotland
PB Power tools
Head office: 29 Long Wood Road, Trafford Park, Manchester
  M17 1PZ; 061-872 6818; branches in Bolton, Liverpool, London,
  Manchester and Tarporley

Do-it-yourself shops

B&Q
DIY Supercentre, Western Avenue, Greenford, Middlesex;
  01-575 7175
Great Mills DIY Superstore
  Highams Park Industrial Estate, Hickman Avenue, Chingford,
  London E4; 01-523 1131; and branches
Payless DIY Ltd
  80 Bushey Road, London SW20; 01-879 7400; and branches
Sainsbury's Homebase
  473 High Road, London NW10; and branches
Texas Homecare DIY Stores
  Head office: Cline Road, London N11; 01-368 0141; and
  branches
WHS Do-it-all Ltd
  138 Bromley Road, London SE6 2UY; 01-461 0101; and
  branches
Wickes DIY Superstores
  53 Plough Lane, London SW17 0BW; 01-947 9817; and
  branches

Some manufacturers and distributors of woodburning stoves

Jotul (Norwegian)
  Sole importers UK and Ireland: Jotul UK Ltd
  Norcem House, Headley Road East, Woodley, Reading
  R65 4SG; 0734 694884
Lange (Danish)
  'Earthworks', 22 Crove Street, Ludlow, Shropshire SY8 1DT;
  0584 2010
Logfires Ltd (English)
  Southern Stoves, South Street, Dorking, Surrey RH4 2HD;
  0306 883201

Foreign property agents

Farrar, Stead & Glyn
  152 Fulham Road, London SW10 9PR; 01-373 8425
Maisons Françaises
  Pantiles Chambers, 85 High Street, Tunbridge Wells,
  Kent TN1 1YG; 0892 48933
Rutherfords
  197 Knightsbridge (4th floor), London SW7 1RB; 01-584 4392
Villotel Ltd
  28 Grafton Terrace, London NW5 4JJ; 01-485 2733

Inside information
Mike and Hugh MacIntyre
  Le Toison d'Or (restaurant), 58 rue du Jerzual, 22100 Dinan,
  Bretagne, France; (010 33) 96 39 32 33. They have contacts with
  local *notaires*.

Further Reading

Buying and selling houses

Do It Yourself Conveyancing, Robert T Steele (David and Charles)
The Legal Side of Buying a House (Consumers' Association)

Grants

Home Improvement Grants: a guide for home owners, landlords
and tenants, Department of the Environment, housing booklet
No 14 (HMSO)

The building regulations

The Building Regulations (HMSO)
The Building Regulations Explained and Illustrated, W S Whyte
and Vincent Powell-Smith (Collins)
Guide to the Building Regulations 1985, A J Elder (Architectural
Press)

General practical information

Alteration or Conversion of Houses, J F Garner (Longman)
Brickwork Repair and Restoration, W G Nash (Attic)
The Complete Home Carpenter, (Orbis)
A Concise Building Encylopaedia, ed. T Corkhill (Pitman)
House and Cottage Conversion: Guide to the Do's and Don'ts,
Hugh Lander (Acanthus Books)
House and Cottage Interiors: Do's and Dont's of, Hugh Lander
(Acanthus Books)
How to Restore a   l Improve Your Victorian House, Alan Johnson
(David and Char   s)
Landscaping (Ti..e-Life Books)
Repairing Houses, Trevor James (Sphere)
The Sunday Times Book of Do-It-Yourself (Sphere)

Heating

Do Your Own Central Heating, Trevor Crabtree (Foulsham)

Layout and decor

The House Book, Terence Conran (Mitchell Beazley)

Architectural styles and historical information

The English Country Cottage, R J Brown (Robert Hale/Hamlyn)
English Farmhouses, R J Brown (Robert Hale/Hamlyn)
How Old is Your House? Pamela Cunnington (Collins)
The Smaller English House: Its History and Development,
Lyndon F Cave
(Robert Hale)
Timber-Framed Buildings of England, R J Brown (Robert Hale)
The Windmills of Hampshire, Anthony Triggs (Milestone)

France

Blue Guide to France, Ian Robertson (A & C Black)
Business Guide to France (Longman)
Fodor Guide to France, Eugene Fodor (Hodder & Stoughton)
France: Information Handbook, Frank Rutherford (Sprucehurst
Ltd, available from Rutherfords, address on page 136)

Further reading from Kogan Page

*Buying for Business: How to Get the Best Deal from Your
Suppliers,* Tony Attwood
The Guardian Guide to Running a Small Business, 7th edn,
Clive Woodcock
Law for the Small Business, 6th edn, Patricia Clayton
Living and Retiring Abroad: The Daily Telegraph Guide,
Michael Furnell, annual
Running Your Own Building Business, Kim Ludman
Running Your Own Estate Agency, Val Redding
The Stoy Hayward Business Tax Guide, annual, Mavis Seymour
and Stephen Say
Understand Your Accounts, 2nd edn, A St J Price
Working for Yourself, 10th edn, Godfrey Golzen

Glossary of technical terms used in the text

Adze. A cutting tool with an arched blade set at right angles to the handle.

Architrave. The ornamental moulding round a door or window opening, usually covering the joint between the plaster and framing.

Bolster. A bricklayer's cutting chisel, with a blade 2 to 5 inches wide.

Cap. A domed top section of a windmill, which rotates on a track, enabling the sails to be turned into the wind.

Cob. A composition of clay, straw, horsehair and stones from which walls are built.

Colonnade. A series of columns forming the side of a narrow covered path outside a building. The columns are bridged by lintels.

Corbel. A projecting support on the face of a wall, often, but not always, decorative as well as functional.

Cornice. A horizontal projecting moulding at the top of framing, or at the junction of wall and ceiling, or on the facade of a building.

Cove. A hollow moulding in the form of a quarter circle or ellipse, often used at the junction of wall and ceiling.

Cruck. A curved timber supporting a roof.

Flashing. Sheet lead, zinc or copper fitted to prevent water from penetrating the joints where a vertical surface, eg a wall of chimney stack, projects through a roof.

Joist. Horizontal timbers which carry the floors and ceilings; traditionally made of wood, but see *RSJ*.

Lintel. A horizontal beam across an opening, usually carrying the wall above. Again, traditionally of wood but now usually reinforced concrete (available ready-made).

Pilaster. A thin, rectangular pier projecting from the face of a wall.

Portico. A porch with its roof supported by columns.

RSJ. A joist made of rolled steel, usually used to support the weight bearing down where a wall has been removed (available ready-made).

Screed. A thin, ie 2 or 3 inch layer of concrete flooring, laid over the main 4 to 6 inches deep concrete floor slab. Pipework and electric cables are concealed in it, and it is trowelled to a smooth finish to receive carpets or floor tiles.

Skirting. A moulded decorative finish between the wall and floor, usually in wood but sometimes in concrete or plaster.

Soaker. A piece of lead or zinc formed into a right angle and bonded with slates or similar to make a watertight joint between a wall and roof. Stepped flashings are used over the soakers.

Tongued and grooved. A form of planking. Each plank has a tongue in one edge and a groove in the other. The tongues and grooves on adjacent planks interlock with each other.

Trompe l'oeil. An architectural or decorative feature designed to deceive the eye. Examples include pilasters and porticos painted on walls to give an illusion of height or distance.

Wainscoting. Wall panelling; also used to refer to skirtings.

Weatherboarding. Thin boards fixed in horizontal overlapping rows to the outside of a building to throw off rainwater and for decorative purposes. A common local feature of architecture in many regions throughout the British Isles.

Index